D0500978

Published by Sellers Publishing, Inc.
81 West Commercial Street
Portland, Maine 04101
For ordering information:
(800) 625-3386 toll free
(207) 772-6814 FAX
Visit our Web site: www.rsvp.com • E-mail: rsp@rsvp.com

Publishing Director: Robin Haywood
Managing Editor: Mary Baldwin
Senior Book Editor: Megan Hiller
Assistant Production Editor: Charlotte Smith
Design: Carol Salvin

Additional Research: Bryce Longton

© 2007 Elizabeth Long
All rights reserved. No part of this book may be reproduced or transmitted in any form, or by any means, without written permission from the publisher, except for the inclusion of brief quotations in reviews.

All trademarks referenced in this book are the property of their respective owners.

ISBN 13: 978-1-56906-985-1
ISBN 10: 1-56906-985-9

DISCLAIMER
Every effort was made to ensure that all the information contained in this book was accurate and up-to-date at the time of publication. The author and the publisher do not warrant the performance, effectiveness, or applicability of any Web sites or resources listed in this publication. This book is meant as a guide to inform and as an organizer for the college application process and in no way guarantees admittance into any college or university.

Printed in China

EVERYTHING YOU NEED TO HELP YOU THROUGH THE COLLEGE APPLICATION PROCESS

ELIZABETH LONG

CONTENTS

INTRODUCTION

Applying to college is a complicated process, and it requires a solid time commitment and a fair amount of effort on your part. From taking the SATs to visiting colleges, to asking teachers to write recommendation letters, to filling out applications and writing essays, there seems to be an endless list of tasks to complete and a mountain of papers to sift through. However, applying to college does not have to be the overwhelming, stressful experience that many applicants make it out to be.

If you are a sophomore or a junior in high school and you are picking up this book for the first time, then you are right on schedule. This book will take you step-by-step through the entire college-admissions process, providing you with to-do lists, scheduling tips and deadline reminders, worksheets, and calendars. Whether you're looking for a college admissions guidebook or want to know which SAT or ACT prep course is right for you, you will find a comprehensive, annotated list of informative resources here. The see-through storage pockets with tabs and checklists found in the back of the book make it easy to organize all of your applications and paperwork.

Chapter 1 guides you through the process of building, researching, and narrowing down your list of colleges until you've compiled your final list of five to eight schools where you will apply. Use the detailed reviews of college guidebooks and online search engines in this chapter to help you get started and focus your search.

The worksheets in Chapter 2 are designed to help you organize your information, including your various activities, experiences, and strengths, in addition to your courses, grades, and test scores. This chapter helps you plan ahead and offers tips on how students can make themselves more appealing to colleges by becoming involved in various activities. You can use the information you generate on these worksheets as a springboard for a possible topic when it comes time to write your essay (a task which stumps many applicants) or for responses to the application's short-answer questions.

The schedules, deadlines, and year-

and semester-specific to-do lists in Chapter 3 will keep you on task in your academic and extracurricular life, as well as make sure you don't forget critical tests or application deadlines.

Chapter 4 will walk you step-by-step through the application process from the all-important essay to the short-answer questions, recommendations, and interview. You'll find definitions for application-related terminology such as early admission, early action, and early acceptance, as well as a helpful discussion of the Common Application and online application options.

Just when you think you've made it through the application process, you have to tackle the financial aid applications.

Chapter 5 reviews all forms of financial aid and takes you through this specific aspect of the college application process, including how to negotiate for more aid once your package comes in.

With the complete **glossary of terms** — including what each term really means for you — and a **quick reference list** of helpful Web sites for all your questions regarding admissions, test prep, and financial aid, you'll never be lost in the college application maze.

The see-through storage pockets with tabs at the back of the book are critical for helping students organize all the paperwork involved in the application process. With a total of eight tabbed pockets, you can use one pocket for each school you apply to, or use extra pockets for financial aid and letters of recommendation materials. Five of the tabbed plastic sleeves provide an application checklist right on the front as an essential reminder of what you must include with each application. You'll find extra-deep pockets at the front and back of the book for any remaining or miscellaneous paperwork.

There are plenty of colleges out there that not only will accept you, but will also make you happy to be spending the next four years of your life there. And there is absolutely no reason why you can't successfully complete the entire college application process with confidence and even learn a thing or two about yourself along the way.

I WANT TO HEAR FROM YOU!

The College Applicant's Organizer can be used by college applicants and their parents as you navigate your way through the college admissions process. I hope that you find this book to be user friendly and filled with helpful information and tips. If you have suggestions on improving certain sections or parts of this book, please let me know. I would also love to know which sections of this book you found to be particularly helpful.

Please e-mail all questions, comments, and suggestions to rsp@RSVP.com.

THIS BOOK BELONGS TO . . .

Name ____________________

Phone ____________________

E-mail ____________________

CHAPTER 1: GETTING STARTED

Deciding where to go to college is incredibly exciting. However, it takes only a quick flip through one of the many college guidebooks to realize just how many schools there are to choose from. For many, the dizzying number of choices can be downright overwhelming.

In this chapter you will find all the information you need to get started with your college search. You can use the college applicant worksheet — which covers everything from the academic environment to the weather — to get you thinking about what factors are important to you as you put together your list of colleges.

You will also find a list of resources that include admissions manuals, which provide information on the actual process, as well as college guidebooks and search engines, which give you information about individual schools.

You will learn about the importance of putting together a balanced list of high-reach, middle-reach, and safety schools. Those of you who have your heart set on an Ivy League college will find a list of companies that help you determine your chances of being accepted as well as counselors and books that deal specifically with admissions to this elite group of schools.

You will also find plenty of tips and information on how to make the most of your experience when you visit colleges. And ultimately, you will have the tools you need to compile a final list of colleges where you wish to apply.

IN THIS CHAPTER

- How to start your college search
    - ✗ College applicant worksheet
    - ✗ Practical considerations
    - ✗ A note to parents
    - ✗ Parent worksheet
- Admission resources
- Finding schools that want you
    - ✗ Plenty of schools to go around
    - ✗ A word about Ivy League admissions
    - ✗ What are your odds?
- Researching colleges
    - ✗ So how do you actually start your search?
    - ✗ School college counselors versus independent college counselors
    - ✗ Online search engines
    - ✗ Comprehensive college guidebooks
    - ✗ Selective college guidebooks
- Visiting colleges
    - ✗ What to do when visiting a school
    - ✗ Once you've been accepted
- Campus considerations
- How to build your list of colleges
    - ✗ Colleges to research worksheet
    - ✗ College overview worksheet
    - ✗ Schools I plan to visit and/or research further worksheet
    - ✗ College applicant worksheet, redux
    - ✗ Parent worksheet, redux
    - ✗ The final list — where I'm applying to college worksheet

HOW TO START YOUR COLLEGE SEARCH

You may already have a list in your mind of where you want to apply to college. Or you may have your heart set on one particular school. Or you may not have the slightest clue as to how to start this process. Regardless of what you're thinking, don't worry. There is a college out there that is a good fit for you — meaning you will be happy attending, and the college will be happy to have you. But in order to find the school that's truly right for you, you need to keep your mind as open as possible as you start (and continue) your college search.

On the following page is a worksheet to get you thinking about what criteria are important to you as you start your search. Fill this out before you get too deep into the research process and your mind becomes too set on any one particular school.

If you do have a clear-cut first choice, take that school out of the equation and assume that it is not an option as you check off the boxes on the worksheet. Don't worry. No one is going to stop you from applying to your first-choice school. The only goal here is to get you thinking about other possibilities.

Also, after each section, you will see the questions "Why?" and "Pros and cons?" Answer these questions as thoroughly as possible. The purpose of asking these questions is to encourage you to think about why you are leaning in a particular direction. If any of your "Why?" answers start with, "Because my mom/dad/brother/best friend/teacher said . . . ," then you should take some time to rethink your answers and figure out what it is that you really want. You are the one who is going to be attending this school, so your opinion is the one that counts here.

One more thing before you get started that will help to put your mind at ease. You are not going to be locked into any of your answers. You can always change your mind. You will find this same worksheet later in the book, so you can see if your answers change after you have done some research and visited some schools.

Chapter 1 Worksheets

Fill out the worksheets in this chapter to begin, refine, and ultimately determine the final list of colleges where you will apply.

college applicant worksheet (pages 11–13):

To get the process started, this worksheet will help you think about what is important to you in a college.

parent worksheet (pages 15–17):

Include your parents in the process early, and get their thoughts by asking them to fill out this worksheet (which is identical to your College Applicant Worksheet).

colleges to research worksheet (pages 31–32):

There are spaces for you to list more than 30 schools on this worksheet. This long list of schools will act as a springboard for deeper research and consideration.

college overview worksheet (pages 33–52):

There are ten copies of this two-page worksheet. Here's where you record the academic and admittance statistics for each college and compare them to your own data. The back side of the College Overview Worksheet will help you compare the offerings of each college to your preferences.

schools I plan to visit and/or research further worksheet (page 53):

There are spaces for ten colleges on this worksheet. Carry over only the colleges that still work for you after you have completed the College Overview Worksheet. This list allows you to record notes and questions you have yet to research.

college applicant worksheet – redux (pages 54–56) and parent worksheet – redux (page 57–59):

These two worksheets are copies of the first worksheets in the chapter. Here's your chance to take what you've learned about what schools offer and weigh it against your own needs and preferences and rethink your choices.

the final list — where I'm applying to college (page 60):

This is it! You've done all your research and found the five to eight schools where you would be happy to spend your college years.

COLLEGE APPLICANT WORKSHEET

If everything else were equal, I would be happiest spending four-plus years at a school . . . (check the appropriate boxes)

environment

- ☐ in a big city
- ☐ in a college town
- ☐ in the suburbs adjacent to a big city
- ☐ in the country
- ☐ no preference

Why? ______________________________

____

____

Pros and cons? ______________________________

____

____

On a scale of 1–5, how important is this?
(circle one) 1 2 3 4 5

weather

- ☐ where it's sunny all the time
- ☐ where you see a change of seasons
- ☐ where the four seasons are rain, hail, sleet, and snow
- ☐ no preference

Why? ______________________________

____

____

Pros and cons? ______________________________

____

____

On a scale of 1–5, how important is this?
(circle one) 1 2 3 4 5

size

- ☐ with fewer than 2,000 undergrads
- ☐ with between 2,000 and 5,000 undergrads
- ☐ with between 5,000 and 10,000 undergrads
- ☐ with between 10,000 and 20,000 undergrads
- ☐ with more than 20,000 undergrads
- ☐ no preference

Why? ______________________________

____

____

Pros and cons? ______________________________

____

____

On a scale of 1–5, how important is this?
(circle one) 1 2 3 4 5

region

- ☐ in the Northeast/Mid-Atlantic states
- ☐ in the Southeast/Gulf states
- ☐ in the Midwest
- ☐ in the Northwest
- ☐ in the Southwest
- ☐ in the West/Pacific Northwest
- ☐ in ______________________________ (city or state)
- ☐ no preference

Why? ______________________________

____

____

Pros and cons? ______________________________

____

____

On a scale of 1–5, how important is this?
(circle one) 1 2 3 4 5

accessibility

- ☐ less than two hours from my family's house
- ☐ two to six hours away
- ☐ less than a day's drive away
- ☐ at least a plane ride away
- ☐ no preference

Why? ______________________________

____

____

Pros and cons? ______________________________

____

____

On a scale of 1–5, how important is this?
(circle one) 1 2 3 4 5

living arrangements

- ☐ where everyone lives in dorms
- ☐ where living in Greek (fraternity/sorority) housing is an option
- ☐ where alternative/theme housing is an option
- ☐ where living off campus is an option
- ☐ where people live with their families and commute
- ☐ no preference

Why? ______________________________

____

____

Pros and cons? ______________________________

____

____

On a scale of 1–5, how important is this?
(circle one) 1 2 3 4 5

Continued on next page

COLLEGE APPLICANT WORKSHEET

social

- ☐ where most of the social scene is on campus
- ☐ where most of the social scene is off campus
- ☐ where weekends revolve around football games
- ☐ where the social scene revolves around the Greek system
- ☐ where there are many extracurricular organizations
- ☐ where weekends are made for road trips
- ☐ where alternative is the norm
- ☐ where the Grateful Dead is still very much alive
- ☐ no preference

Why? ______________________

Pros and cons? ______________________

On a scale of 1–5, how important is this?
(circle one) 1 2 3 4 5

culture

- ☐ where you can hear live music
- ☐ where you can visit museums
- ☐ where you can see live theater
- ☐ where watching football is considered a cultural outing
- ☐ where you can eat out at nice restaurants
- ☐ where you can shop

Why? ______________________

Pros and cons? ______________________

On a scale of 1–5, how important is this?
(circle one) 1 2 3 4 5

politics

- ☐ where students are conservative
- ☐ where students are liberal
- ☐ where students do not define themselves by their politics
- ☐ where religion plays a role in daily life
- ☐ no preference

Why? ______________________

Pros and cons? ______________________

On a scale of 1–5, how important is this?
(circle one) 1 2 3 4 5

academics

- ☐ where studying is everything and students fight for their class rank
- ☐ where students take their classes very seriously but the environment isn't quite so competitive
- ☐ where students are invested in their studies but academics don't rule their lives
- ☐ where showing up for class is not a requirement to pass

Sorry, "no preference" is not an option on this one. You have to make a decision here.

Why? ______________________

Pros and cons? ______________________

On a scale of 1–5, how important is this?
(circle one) 1 2 3 4 5

COLLEGE APPLICANT WORKSHEET

ADDITIONAL THOUGHTS (Use this space to note other criteria you want to consider as you put together your list.)

Practical considerations

Hopefully, in the process of filling out the previous worksheet, you were able to get a sense of what you are looking for in a school. Depending on your answers, there may or may not be one single school that will perfectly meet all of your wishes. But you should now have a clearer sense of the factors that are really important to you as well as those on which you are more flexible.

How great it would be if this were all it took for you to figure out where you want to go to college! Unfortunately, there are other more practical factors to consider when determining what schools go on your list. In short order, these are:

- Are your parents okay with this choice?
- What are your chances of being accepted?
- Can you afford the tuition? If not, will you qualify for financial aid?

getting your parents on board

It is a good idea to sit down with your parents now and find out what sort of parameters they intend to set regarding your choice of college. Hopefully, your parents will be as open-minded as you are, but if they have hard and fast rules, it's better that you find them out now rather than later, after you've completed the application, written the essays, and set your heart on a particular school. (If your parents do have rules, ask them to explain their reasons. Often, once you hear what they have to say, it becomes easier to accept their rules.)

Ask your parents to take a few minutes to fill out the Parent Worksheet (which is identical to the one you just filled out). Then give them the time and the space they need to fill the worksheet out on their own. This is not the time for you to stand over their shoulders and feed them the answers you want to hear. Once they've finished filling out the worksheet, ask them to sit down with you so that you can compare your answers.

There is always the possibility that your parents' answers will be completely different from yours. If this is the case, ask them to explain why they chose the answers they did. Then ask them to give you the opportunity to explain your reasons for your answers. Your answers to the "Why?" and "Pros and cons?" questions will come in very handy here.

Most likely, deciding where to go to college is one of the first really big decisions you will make. As exciting as this is to you — and it should be a huge thrill — your parents may find the whole experience at least a little stressful. No matter what your parents' response, this is not the time for huffing, puffing, shouting, and slamming doors. You are on the verge of adulthood. Even if your parents are behaving a little less rationally than you would like, take this opportunity to show them that you are approaching this decision in a grown-up fashion. You'll get much farther that way.

A note to parents

The worksheet on the following page is identical to the worksheet filled out by your child. You may check as many boxes in each section as you wish.

If you have a clear-cut first choice for your child's college, take that school out of the equation and assume that it is not an option. Don't worry. No one is going to stop you from encouraging your child to apply to that school. The only goal here is to get you thinking about other possibilities for your son or daughter.

When you're finished, you and your child should sit down and compare answers. Keep in mind that your son's or daughter's answers may be completely different from your own. No matter how strongly you feel about a particular issue, keep an open mind and try not to be critical of your child's answers. When you disagree, explain your reasons and ask your son or daughter to do the same. The old standby "Because I'm your parent and I said so" is not the way to resolve matters in this situation.

If your child begins to act irrationally, remember that this is the first big "adult" decision your teenager has been faced with. He or she could be freaking out for any number of reasons, including anxiety about leaving home, angst about getting into the right college, or simply self-conciousness because someone at school gave him or her a funny look. Your teen is on the verge of adulthood, and sometimes, the more a teenager wants to be taken seriously as an adult, the more childishly he or she behaves. So, hang in there and be patient. You all will get through this.

One final note before you get started: the fact that you loved or hated your college experience does not mean the same will hold true for your teenager. It may be hard, but try to keep an open mind and remember to focus on what's best for your child.

PARENT WORKSHEET

If everything else were equal, I would be happiest seeing my son/daughter spend four-plus years at a school . . . (check the appropriate boxes)

environment

- ☐ in a big city
- ☐ in a college town
- ☐ in the suburbs adjacent to a big city
- ☐ in the country
- ☐ no preference

Why? ______________________

____

____

Pros and cons? ______________________

____

____

On a scale of 1–5, how important is this?
(circle one) 1 2 3 4 5

weather

- ☐ where it's sunny all the time
- ☐ where you see a change of seasons
- ☐ where the four seasons are rain, hail, sleet, and snow
- ☐ no preference

Why? ______________________

____

____

Pros and cons? ______________________

____

____

On a scale of 1–5, how important is this?
(circle one) 1 2 3 4 5

size

- ☐ with fewer than 2,000 undergrads
- ☐ with between 2,000 and 5,000 undergrads
- ☐ with between 5,000 and 10,000 undergrads
- ☐ with between 10,000 and 20,000 undergrads
- ☐ with more than 20,000 undergrads
- ☐ no preference

Why? ______________________

____

____

Pros and cons? ______________________

____

____

On a scale of 1–5, how important is this?
(circle one) 1 2 3 4 5

region

- ☐ in the Northeast/Mid-Atlantic states
- ☐ in the Southeast/Gulf states
- ☐ in the Midwest
- ☐ in the Northwest
- ☐ in the Southwest
- ☐ in the West/Pacific Northwest
- ☐ in ______________________ (city or state)
- ☐ no preference

Why? ______________________

____

____

Pros and cons? ______________________

____

____

On a scale of 1–5, how important is this?
(circle one) 1 2 3 4 5

accessibility

- ☐ less than two hours from my family's house
- ☐ two to six hours away
- ☐ less than a day's drive away
- ☐ at least a plane ride away
- ☐ no preference

Why? ______________________

____

____

Pros and cons? ______________________

____

____

On a scale of 1–5, how important is this?
(circle one) 1 2 3 4 5

living arrangements

- ☐ where everyone lives in dorms
- ☐ where living in Greek (fraternity/sorority) housing is an option
- ☐ where alternative/theme housing is an option
- ☐ where living off campus is an option
- ☐ where people live with their families and commute
- ☐ no preference

Why? ______________________

____

____

Pros and cons? ______________________

____

____

On a scale of 1–5, how important is this?
(circle one) 1 2 3 4 5

Continued on next page

PARENT WORKSHEET

social

- ☐ where most of the social scene is on campus
- ☐ where most of the social scene is off campus
- ☐ where weekends revolve around football games
- ☐ where the social scene revolves around the Greek system
- ☐ where there are many extracurricular organizations
- ☐ where weekends are made for road trips
- ☐ where alternative is the norm
- ☐ where the Grateful Dead is still very much alive
- ☐ no preference

Why? ______________________

____

____

Pros and cons? ______________________

____

____

On a scale of 1–5, how important is this?
(circle one) 1 2 3 4 5

culture

- ☐ where you can hear live music
- ☐ where you can visit museums
- ☐ where you can see live theater
- ☐ where watching football is considered a cultural outing
- ☐ where you can eat out at nice restaurants
- ☐ where you can shop

Why? ______________________

____

____

Pros and cons? ______________________

____

____

On a scale of 1–5, how important is this?
(circle one) 1 2 3 4 5

politics

- ☐ where students are conservative
- ☐ where students are liberal
- ☐ where students do not define themselves by their politics
- ☐ where religion plays a role in daily life
- ☐ no preference

Why? ______________________

____

____

Pros and cons? ______________________

____

____

On a scale of 1–5, how important is this?
(circle one) 1 2 3 4 5

academics

- ☐ where studying is everything and students fight for their class rank
- ☐ where students take their classes very seriously but the environment isn't quite so competitive
- ☐ where students are invested in their studies but academics don't rule their lives
- ☐ where showing up for class is not a requirement to pass

Sorry, "no preference" is not an option on this one. You have to make a decision here.

Why? ______________________

____

____

Pros and cons? ______________________

____

____

On a scale of 1–5, how important is this?
(circle one) 1 2 3 4 5

PARENT WORKSHEET

ADDITIONAL THOUGHTS (Use this space to note other criteria you want to consider as you put together your list.)

Admission resources

For more information on the admissions process, check out the following titles:

Admission Matters: What Students and Parents Need to Know About Getting Into College
Jossey-Bass ($14.95)
This book is, to put it plainly, excellent. It reads well for both students and parents, and covers all sorts of information. You'll find out why the SAT changed and why colleges are so competitive these days. The book also does an excellent job of dispelling college myths (for example, that going to an elite university will net you a heftier paycheck once you graduate).
FINAL WORD: A good book for parents and teenagers alike.

Barron's The All-In-One College Guide: A More-Results, Less-Stress Plan for Choosing, Getting Into, Finding the Money for, and Making the Most out of College
Barron's ($12.99)
Written by Marty Nemko, an expert in both the getting-into-college and making-the-most-of-life arenas, *The All-In-One College Guide* is part college-admission manual and part self-help book. It covers just about everything from deciding between two-year and four-year colleges to where to get help if you have an eating disorder. It includes an excellent, albeit light, overview of the admissions process and handy tips for those lost in a sea of applications, brand-name schools, and financial aid forms. The chapter on tuition includes information on the best way to go about borrowing for college, tips on how to keep your 529 plan from counting against you when you ask for aid, and a list of the "Best Values in Higher Education."
FINAL WORD: A quick, easy read with plenty of tips.

Cracking College Admissions
The Princeton Review ($15.95)
This basic review of the college admissions process does a solid job of outlining the path from registering for standardized tests to submitting your application to paying for the college of your choice. It covers SAT testing tips, grades, extracurricular activities, applications, essays, early admissions, and financial aid. This is a good primer for those with lots of questions on the actual process. And for those who like knowing what not to do, you'll find plenty of information on the pitfalls to avoid.
FINAL WORD: A good starter manual.

Don't Worry, You'll Get In: 100 Winning Tips for Stress-Free College Admissions
Marlowe & Company ($14.95)
Cowritten by Michele Hernãndez and parenting expert Mimi Doe, this book addresses the two sides of the competitive college admissions game. On the left-side pages Hernãndez deftly handles the admissions process and how to navigate it most effectively, while Doe covers the emotional side of the process on the right-side pages with tips on how to manage stress. Unless you are looking for just the facts, this integrated approach will be well worth your time, offering valuable insight into everything from how to choose the right school to how to manage your nerves when taking the SATs.
FINAL WORD: Good advice on how to cope emotionally with the stress of college admissions.

The Truth About Getting In: A Top College Advisor Tells You Everything You Need to Know
Hyperion ($21.95)
Ivywise founder Katherine Cohen's outline of the steps required to successfully apply to college has brought many a college-bound senior back from the brink of a full-blown panic attack. Each chapter in this admissions manual includes sections titled "Myths and Truths," and "Insider Tips," which help applicants cut through the hype and hearsay surrounding the admissions process. Cohen also covers "the brag sheet." And she gives the lowdown on private counselors while also offering tips on how to get the most out of working with your college counselor. The chapters "Choosing Your College" and "Selling Yourself" are also well worth the read.
FINAL WORD: A great book for decoding the process.

> I wasted a lot of time and energy on a school that was a no-go for my parents from the start. If they had just told me the truth — that with three kids in college at the same time they couldn't afford the tuition plus all the plane tickets back and forth — I would have understood.
>
> *— Meredith, Portland, Ore.*

FINDING SCHOOLS THAT WANT YOU

For whatever reason (call it human nature), the vast majority of applicants seem to set their sights on a school that is either a high-reach, just out of reach, or completely unattainable. The colleges do absolutely nothing to help the situation. In fact, they fuel applicants' unrealistic expectations by encouraging as many students as possible to apply to their school. Why? Because the more applicants it has, the better the college looks.

Ask guidance counselors or admissions officers the cause of this phenomenon, and they are likely to point the finger at the rankings generated by *U.S. News & World Report*. However, as much as the colleges gripe about these rankings, they are quick to celebrate when they move up a spot or two on the list.

To say that the system is spiraling out of control is an understatement. The more applications a college brings in, the higher it ranks, which only serves to bring in even more applications the next year, which in turn pushes the college even higher up in the ranking system.

Plenty of schools to go around

Yes, it's true. The college admissions process has become much more competitive in recent years. However, the bulk of the competition lies within a small circle of elite schools that have garnered name-brand appeal. Not getting into one of these colleges does not mean you are destined to an education full of night classes. On the contrary, you will still have plenty of excellent colleges to choose from.

There are well over 1,000 four-year colleges in the United States. The major comprehensive college guides cover all or most of these schools. Of the schools, only 100 (or fewer by some calculations) admit less than 50 percent of their applicant pool. Many of the remaining 900-plus schools listed in the guides have space available right up until the school year starts in the fall.

Another alternative to investigate is a two-year school or community college. There are benefits to this approach, the major one being that you can save a considerable amount of money while exploring career interests. If you choose this route and plan on transferring to a four-year school, there are a few things to consider:

- Speak with a college counselor at the community college about preparing for and meeting requirements for transfer.
- Ask which classes will prepare you for entry into an upper-division college.
- Make sure all credits will be transferable.
- Investigate articulation agreements (if any) between the two-year school you plan to attend and four-year schools — this type of agreement often makes transferring much smoother.

So the good news is you have nothing to worry about. There is, unquestionably, a college out there that wants you. However, you have to choose wisely when deciding where to apply. It will not do you any good to apply to ten backup schools if all of them are high-reach or out of reach for you.

What's the difference between a high-reach, a middle-reach and a safety school?

- A **high-reach school** is one in which you fall in the bottom 30 percent of applicants.
- A **middle-reach school** is one in which you are in the middle 40 percent of applicants. You are more likely to receive a better financial aid package at a middle-reach school.
- A **safety school** is one in which you sit in the top 30 percent of applicants. You are more likely to be admitted into honors programs at a safety school and receive the best financial aid package.

You should apply to a wide enough range of schools that you have at least three on your final list from the combined middle-reach or safety categories.

It is absolutely essential that you put just as much thought into deciding which schools to apply to in the middle-reach and safety categories as you do for your high-reach schools. Depending on how much of a reach your high-reach schools are, there is always the chance that you will wind up at one of your middle-reach or safety choices. And often, when it comes time to write the tuition check, students go with a safety school even though they were accepted by their high- or middle-reach schools, simply because they received a better financial aid package from their safety school.

If your grades, test scores, and extracurriculars all fall within the same top 30 percent, middle 40 percent, or bottom 30 percent, you will have no problem determining which category a school is for you. Unfortunately, more often than not, your grades will put you in one category, your test scores in another, and your extracurriculars in a third. Without knowing exactly how much weight is given to each of these elements (and this is not information colleges reveal), it's tough to figure out what your chances are.

NOTES

A word about Ivy League admissions

Given the large numbers of qualified applicants and the limited number of spaces, all of the Ivy League schools should be considered high-reach schools for all applicants (unless you have a very tangible hook, such as you are being recruited or your mom donated the new wing to the library). In many cases, applicants who scored 2400 on the SAT or were class valedictorians have not been accepted by any of these schools. You may be a perfectly qualified, or even overqualified, applicant. There is still no guarantee that you will be accepted by your first, second, third, fourth, fifth, sixth, seventh, or even eighth choice among the Ivy League colleges. There is really no telling what will happen when you apply to these schools. No one is suggesting you not apply. But unless you are accepted early action/decision, you need to apply to middle-reach and safety choices outside the Ivy League.

the elusive Ivies

- Brown University
- Columbia University
- Cornell University
- Dartmouth College
- Harvard University
- Princeton University
- University of Pennsylvania
- Yale University

they're not Ivy but they may as well be

- Amherst College
- Barnard College
- Boston College
- Bowdoin College
- California Institute of Technology
- UC–Berkeley
- University of Chicago
- Claremont College
- Colby College
- Colgate University
- College of William and Mary
- Columbia College
- Duke University
- Georgetown University
- Johns Hopkins University
- Massachusetts Institute of Technology (MIT)
- Middlebury College
- Northwestern University
- University of Notre Dame
- New York University
- Pomona College
- Rice University
- Stanford University
- Swarthmore College
- Trinity University
- Tufts University
- Vassar College
- Wesleyan University
- Williams College

What are your odds?

Go 4 Ivy

www.go4ivy.com

If you're looking for a crystal ball to tell you whether or not you'll get into the colleges on your list, check out the ChancesR program on this Web site. The program calculates your chances of admission by evaluating specific criteria — beyond test scores and GPAs — to determine whether an applicant's qualities match up with the qualities a college is seeking. This service is best for applicants who cannot determine whether a school is a high-reach, middle-reach, or safety, often because of a disparity in grades and test scores. The cost for a search is $14.95 per college, or you can get a package deal of 20 colleges for $224.25. It covers only 150 colleges, albeit the top 150, where the chances of admission are the hardest to gauge.

Thick Envelope

www.thickenvelope.com

Another option for those who want to know their odds at specific schools is thickenvelope.com. Founded by Harvard grads Richard Sorenson and Grant Ujifusa, (both of whom are also the proud dads of Harvard undergrads), this site covers only 100 of the top schools in the United States, but it's a pretty good deal at $7.95 for a single college analysis or $89.95 for all 100 (plus a $9.95 repeat-access usage fee). In addition to grades, class rank, curriculum, SAT scores, and extracurriculars, the analysis includes an exhaustive list of questions to think about when choosing the teachers who will be writing your recommendations.

When only Ivy will do

Hernāndez College Consulting

www.hernandezcollegeconsulting.com

Imagine spending upwards of $30,000 to hire someone who will do everything in her power to make it look as if she isn't working for you. Intrigued? Meet college counselor extraordinaire Michele Hernāndez, who spent four years as the assistant director of admissions at Dartmouth College. Dr. Hernāndez works one-on-one with her clients, providing applicants with her expertise — and unlimited time! — every step of the way. Her services include, but are not limited to, interview prep, application assistance, advice on how to spend your summer vacation, what you need to put on your required reading list, and how to decide where to go once you've gotten your acceptance letters. She starts working with students as early as the eighth grade and as late as the tenth grade. Because Hernāndez offers such an extraordinary level of service to her clients, she is able to accommodate only a limited number of students. If you're too late to get in on, or can't afford, one of her consulting packages, check out her College Application Boot Camp. (See page 108 for more information.)

FINAL WORD: If you can afford her and she has space to take you, she delivers.

Ivywise

www.ivywise.com

Featured in *Vogue* and *New York* magazines, *The Wall Street Journal*, and *The New York Times*, Ivywise is the real deal. Ivywise's founder, Katherine Cohen, PhD, graduated from both Brown and Yale. Her team of admissions counselors graduated from Brown, Northwestern, Brandeis, U Penn, and Vassar to name a few. Ivywise helps students find and get into the school that is the right fit for them, offering a myriad of services from nursery school admittance(!) all the way up to graduate school. According to the Web site, 90 percent of the company's students are admitted to one of their top two choices, and 100 percent of Ivywise's students are admitted to one of their top three choices. The tip sections are really helpful. Information includes the most common (and worst) essay topics (declarations of love for your boy/girlfriend is on the list). The company even offers pro bono consulting for those who can't afford Ivywise's sky-high $30,000+ price tag.

FINAL WORD: If you are in the market for a consultant, this one's worth a look.

Can't fathom spending more than a year's worth of tuition on a college counselor?

A Is for Admission: The Insider's Guide to Getting Into the Ivy League and Other Top Colleges

Warner Books ($14.95)

Many consider this book to be the final word in Ivy League admissions. You'll find an easy-to-understand explanation of the Academic Index — the official system Ivy League colleges use to rank applicants, plus plenty of insider information on everything from the real weight SATs carry at these schools to why not to hold your breath if you get waitlisted. You will also learn the reasons, according to the book's author Michele Hernāndez (see Hernāndez College Consulting, this page), to attend an Ivy League school — getting a brand-name diploma shouldn't be one of them.

FINAL WORD: If you want to get into the Ivy League, get this book.

College Confidential

www.collegeconfidential.com (free!)*

Another big player in the high-priced college-counseling arena is College Confidential. College Confidential distinguishes itself by providing an abundance of information free online, with no site registration required. College counseling services range from the reasonably priced stats eval ($89) and essay evaluation ($250) to the Ivy Guaranteed Admissions Program ($15,000), which guarantees those accepted into the program admittance to one of their top two schools. Admissions counselor Dave Berry and admissions officer David Hawsey, authors of *Princeton Review: America's Elite Colleges*, are the brains behind this organization.

FINAL WORD: This Web site is a phenomenal resource, even if you don't have the funds or the inclination to spend money on college counseling services.

*There are other services on this site that are not free.

> If I had it to do over, I would have been more methodical about deciding where to apply [to college]. In hindsight, my choices were all pretty arbitrary.
>
> —*Shannon, Boulder, Col.*

RESEARCHING COLLEGES

So how do you actually start your search?

- Sit down with your college counselor and review your academic record as well as your aspirations. Then get a list of suggestions of colleges to research.
- Go online — Princeton Review and the College Board, among others, offer free college search engines. (See online college search engine reviews on this page.)
- Go to the bookstore or library and pick up one of the college guides — the *Fiske Guide to Colleges* is outstanding. (See college guidebook reviews on pages 24–25.)
- Talk to friends who already attend college and ask what they think of their school as well as other schools they considered.
- If you come across a college in your travels, stop and take a look. Even if it's not a potential school, it may give you ideas about what you want (or don't want) to look for in a college.

School college counselors versus independent college counselors

Your school college counselor is a good person to get to know. In addition to advising you with college selection and planning, he or she can also help you with your applications. Unfortunately, as helpful as your counselor may want to be, because you are one of many students (depending on the size of your school) needing help, you may not get as much attention as you require. Often, your counselor has little time to gather firsthand knowledge of various schools by visiting them or meeting with college officials. This means that ultimately it's going to be up to you to find out which schools will be the best match for you. If you're looking for firsthand (and first-rate) knowledge from a specialist — and money is not an issue — then an independent college counselor is the way to go. Independent counselors are especially valuable for students who hope to attend a highly selective school. Less motivated students who need extra help finding a school that, while less competitive, will provide them with a quality education will also benefit from an independent counselor. As an added bonus, independent counselors are available year-round, while school counselors can help you only during the academic year.

TIP: You may have been assigned an academic adviser or homeroom teacher, independent of your college counselor, whom you can consult about your curriculum. If this is the case, you may want to consult this person, in addition to your college counselor, whenever you are advised in this book to talk to your college counselor.

Online college search engines

Princeton Review – Counselor-o-matic (free!)
www.princetonreview.com
If you prefer performing your college search online, then this Web site is worth checking out. First you answer questions on a variety of subjects, including your grades, class rank, curriculum, test scores, extracurriculars, how much you can spend on tuition, as well as what you are looking for in a college and a campus. Then Princeton Review's Counselor-o-matic churns out a list of schools that fit your profile, broken down into the high, good match, and safety categories. This interactive program is great for providing you with a preliminary list, but some of the schools it puts in the high category may be so high as to be completely out of the realm of possibility.
FINAL WORD: A great way to jumpstart your search.

Destination U
www.destinationu.com
It's not free, in fact it's a whopping $199.95. However, it's not the worst thing to spend money on in your college search. The personality test matches you with schools that are a good fit for you, not your resumē. Founded by college counselor Toby Waldorf and her venture capitalist son, Destination U takes the same approach as the dating service eharmony.com, which matches people based on personality traits. In this case, you are being matched to a college.
FINAL WORD: If you're a fan of personality tests, this is for you.

Comprehensive college guidebooks

These comprehensive, A-to-Z college guidebooks are a great place to start if you have absolutely no idea where you want to go to school or what you want in a school. Given the breadth of information covered in these books, the details are scant.

Barron's Profiles of American Colleges

Barron's Educational Series ($28.99)
Covering more than 1,650 accredited colleges in 1,680 pages, this is a whopper of a book. In this book, Barron's covers mostly statistics handed out by the colleges themselves — admissions requirements, extracurricular activities, and library facilities — and ranks schools according to Barron's scale of "noncompetitive to most competitive." It also comes with a CD-Rom with most of the same information on it.
FINAL WORD: Check it out of a library.

College Board College Handbook

College Board ($28.95)
If you can get past the fact that the College Board is the creator of the SAT, you'll find this book contains an abundance of information. Covering all accredited schools in the United States, it is definitely one of the most comprehensive college guides on the market. While the *College Handbook* tends to present just the facts, it is not so dry as, say, reading comprehension passages from a certain standardized test. Another plus is the exhaustive categorical indexes, which help students sort out schools based on their individual criteria, making it a great tool for students starting the search process.
FINAL WORD: A great place to start. It's worth a trip to the library.

The Princeton Review: Complete Book of Colleges

The Princeton Review ($26.95)
An A-to-Z (as opposed to state-by-state) reference, this gargantuan book, which is updated annually, is heavy on stats. Each of the 1,774 college profiles includes admission requirements, financial aid information, student/faculty ratios, and housing options. Unlike PR's *The 361 Best Colleges*, which is filled with fun facts, this doesn't have much personal information within the listings for each school. Beware: Princeton Review does not generate the content on the last 500 pages of the book. It's pay-to-be-listed editorial-type advertising written by the colleges.
FINAL WORD: A starter guide.

U.S. News & World Reports: Ultimate College Guide

Sourcebooks ($26.95)
An almost dizzying dictionary of college profiles, the *U.S. News Ultimate College Guide* is considered by many to be the final word in college rankings. And if you want to know how schools measure up, this book — with just under 100 pages of rankings on subjects like selectivity, freshmen retention rates, and financial aid — is a must. The majority of this six-and-a-half-pound, 1,767-page behemoth of a book that is updated annually is comprised of one-page rundowns of U.S. colleges. Each entry contains a list of stats (SAT scores, tuition, admission rates) and degrees offered, plus information on tuition/financial aid, and campus life, (housing, clubs, Greek life). This guide also contains an exhaustive index of which schools offer which majors — with everything from anthropology to food science to mechanical engineering to philosophy accounted for.
FINAL WORD: It's a great reference.

Selective college guidebooks — top 300 to 400 schools

Fiske Guide to Colleges

Sourcebooks, Inc ($22.95)
Created by Edward B. Fiske, the former education editor for *the New York Times*, the *Fiske* guide, which is updated annually, is a great one. You'll find all sorts of pertinent information in the introduction, including a list of the "Best Buys" (public and private), schools with pre-professional programs, and the best schools for students with learning disabilities. The main part of this book — and the reason everyone buys it — is *Fiske's* review of more than 300 colleges and universities. The reviews, which run about two pages each, offer an informed, balanced look at each school. And while schools do receive academic, social, and quality-of-life ratings, this book is refreshingly free of the cutthroat ranking/tier system you find in some other guides. Another very useful feature is the Overlaps, which list the other schools most frequently applied to by applicants of each school.
FINAL WORD: If you only buy one book, this is the one to buy.

(continued)

The Insider's Guide to the Colleges

St. Martin's Griffin ($19.99)

This down-to-earth guide, compiled and edited by the staff of *The Yale Daily News*, relies on interviews with students to create its college profiles. As a result, you get an insider look at campuses that has not been filtered through colleges' PR machine. *The Insider's Guide* covers 320 schools, dedicating approximately two pages to each school. This book doesn't deliver all of the stats one would expect from a college guide — SAT and ACT test scores are noticeably absent. But it does deliver on entertaining items like "The Insider Top-Ten Lists," which include such rankings as "Unique Mascots" and "Preppiest Student Bodies." The FYI at the end of each profile does a good job of delivering the bottom line on each school. **FINAL WORD:** The inside view is priceless, but for admissions data you'll need to look elsewhere.

The Princeton Review: The Best 361 Colleges: The Smart Student's Guide to Colleges, 2007 Edition

Random House ($21.95)

SAT coaching services notwithstanding, Princeton Review is probably most famous for its college ranking system, which is much better received than (although perhaps not taken quite as seriously as) the rankings generated by *U.S. News and World Report*. There are five separate rankings under party schools alone. You'll also find the requisite academic rankings, as well as worthwhile rankings on demographics and quality of life. While the 361 schools listed in this book may not be the definitive list of the 361 best colleges, the book does a pretty decent job of making the case that these are, in fact, the ones you should be looking at. With two pages allotted for each school on the list, each college/university is given a good shakedown. **FINAL WORD:** It's as entertaining as it is informative.

The Princeton Review: Visiting College Campuses

Princeton Review ($20.00)

If you are the type who likes to be extra prepared when you travel, you may want to bring this book along on your visits. It covers 250 campuses and offers maps, campus highlights, and tour times (confirm times before you go). This book would be most handy for those without access to the Internet, since most of this information is available on the Web sites of the colleges you wish to visit. It does, however give some interesting tidbits regarding each college town. **FINAL WORD:** If you like travel guides, you'll like this book.

The Princeton Review: America's Best Value Colleges

The Princeton Review ($18.95)

This book profiles 150 schools that are just enough under the radar to still be a good value. The first 60 pages give an overview of the nonmonetary factors you need to think about when choosing a school (location, campus size, social activities, etc). You will also find the usual advice on subjects such as applying for financial aid and getting good grades to qualify for scholarships. This book distinguishes itself from the pack by showing students money-saving strategies such as transferring from a junior college, joining the armed forces, and/or taking a year off to work and save money. The comprehensive three-page listings of each school include stats like retention, gender, ethnicity, admissions, and popular majors. There is also a good description of campus life — social activities and rigors of academia — and the all-important bang-for-your-buck factor.
FINAL WORD: If you're serious about saving money on tuition, it's worth spending money on this.

Collegiate Choice

www.collegiatechoice.com

This Web site offers unedited home movie-type "Walking Tour Videos" that are, despite the name, formatted on DVD. You can check out more than 250 schools without even leaving your home. At $15 a piece, the DVDs range in length from 30 minutes to two hours. You are certainly not going to get as clear a picture as you would by checking out a school in person. However, you will definitely get a more honest view than you would from a promotional video distributed by the college. Graphically, the Web site is bare-bones. But even if you aren't interested in the Walking Tours, it's worth checking this site out for the amusing links. Highlights include "favorite recommendation and rejection letters." Also worth looking at is the "worst college interview ever," in which some poor applicant thought he was meeting with an alum from Yale when he was in fact talking to a Harvard grad.
FINAL WORD: This site is the next best thing to visiting the colleges.

VISITING COLLEGES

Most applicants visit colleges starting in the spring of their junior year and continue through the winter and spring of their senior year, sometimes right up until they are forced to make a decision in May.

The more schools you can visit the better. Starting in the tenth grade, anytime you go on a family outing or trip, check to see which colleges are in the vicinity and visit them if they look even remotely interesting. It's best to visit colleges when class is in session. While most schools offer summer classes, attendance is significantly lower at this time than during the fall and spring semesters, so it doesn't give you a full sense of what the school is like. But if this is the only time of year you can visit, it beats doing a cyber tour from your living room sofa.

When you visit schools, try to do as many things as possible from the suggestions below that are appropriate for your age. Keep in mind, the closer you are to attending a school, the more involved your visit should be. While it would be good for a senior to spend the night in a dorm at a school he or she is seriously considering, this wouldn't be appropriate for a high-school freshman.

What to do when visiting a school

take a tour of the campus (appropriate for all grades)

It is a good idea to take a student-led tour to get an overview of a campus. At the very least you will learn where the classrooms, student center, cafeteria, library, auditorium, athletic center, theater, and art studios are located, as well as some historical information about the campus. While you will have the opportunity to ask questions, you should keep in mind that the tour guide's job is to show you the school and present the campus in a positive light. Your tour guide is not in a position to give you the lowdown, so think twice before asking questions that may make your tour guide uncomfortable. Keeping in mind that you may get the party line, you may want to ask the following list of questions of your tour guide:

- How would you describe the academic environment?
- What are the most popular majors/courses?
- Which department has the reputation of having the best professors?
- How accessible are professors to students? Are professors available to help students outside of classroom hours?
- How difficult is it for students to get the courses they want in the [fill in the blank] department?
- How difficult is it to get into courses as a freshman, sophomore, junior, or senior?
- Are sophomores, juniors, and seniors guaranteed a dorm room if they want it? Do most students live off campus after freshman year?
- What is the percentage of students active in the Greek system (fraternities and sororities)?
- What are the most popular social activities for non-Greek students?
- What are the most popular off-campus activities for students?
- What types of intramural sports are offered?

go where your interests lie (appropriate for all grades)

Check out departments that are of particular interest to you. This is another opportunity for you to see if you can imagine yourself happily existing among the students at a particular school. For example, if you know you plan to major in drama, be sure to check out the theater school. Take the time to find out where drama majors hang out and spend some time among them so that you can get a sense of who your classmates will be. Likewise, if you plan to major in English or to attend the business school, check out the English department or the business school and seek out students in those majors.

hang out in the student center around lunchtime (appropriate for all grades)

This is your opportunity to get a good look at the general student population to see if you can imagine yourself happily mingling among them. If you are looking for the lowdown on a school, students are the ones to ask. Most students will be more than happy to answer your questions if you tell them that you are thinking about applying to their school. Following are some of the questions you may want to ask students when you visit a school:

- What do you think of the [fill in the blank] department?
- Which departments is the school best known for?
- Does the school meet your expectations academically, socially, in the arts, etc.?
- What are typical social activities at the school?
- What is your favorite/least favorite thing about the school?

- Knowing what you know now, if you had it to do over, would you attend this school? Why or why not?

stick your head in the admissions office (appropriate for all grades)

It never hurts to let the admissions office at a school know that you are interested. And while asking questions definitely expresses your interest, you want to make a good impression, so think twice before asking obvious questions that can be easily answered by visiting a college's Web site. Freshman, sophomores, and even juniors can get away with asking more obvious questions than seniors can.

eat a meal on campus (appropriate for all grades)

In addition to giving you another opportunity to get a sense of the students, this is also an opportunity to check out the food on campus. (Some schools may not permit you to eat a meal on campus until after you have been accepted.)

have an interview (appropriate for 11th and 12th graders only)

Once you kick your college search into high gear in the spring of your junior year, you should schedule an interview (when possible) at each college you visit.

Once you've been accepted

While colleges certainly make every effort to welcome all potential applicants, they really roll out the red carpet for students who have been accepted. You will often be given the opportunity to speak to (and stay with) a current student, attend classes, and talk to teachers. Your decision is going to directly affect the next four years of your life, so take advantage of all of these opportunities.

spend a night on campus

Spending a night in the dorm provides you with a great opportunity to experience student life firsthand. If you have a friend or a friend of a friend you can stay with in the dorm, that is your best bet. If not, contact the admissions office. Whenever possible, your admissions officer will be more than happy to set up an overnight visit for you. By all means, you should have fun when you visit — but use good judgment. And make sure you take a cell phone or calling card number and have someone you can contact if you have a problem. Also, bring a sleeping bag and pillow — you will most likely be sleeping on the floor.

sit in on classes

If you know you want to get a degree in architecture, then you definitely ought to sit in on a couple of architecture classes. If possible, sit in on one lecture and one smaller class in your area(s) of interest. It is also a good idea to sit in on one of the required freshman courses, such as English.

talk to professors

This is your opportunity to get answers to any remaining questions you have. Be respectful of the professors' time and avoid asking questions that can easily be answered by reading the college's course catalog.

CAMPUS CONSIDERATIONS

public versus private

You may have heard your parents gripe about taxes once or twice over the years. Since a portion of those tax dollars goes to public universities, this is your opportunity to put those dollars to work. If you live in the state, you get resident tuition rates. Often, you also get preference over non-residents when it comes to admission. And if you're the type of person who loves diversity — both in friends and curriculum — you'll find much to choose from at public schools. But if you think three — let alone 3,000 — is a crowd and you already have a very specific idea of the type of curriculum you'd like to study, then you'll probably be happier at a private college. Funded entirely on tuition, fees, private gifts, and endowments, private colleges are more expensive. But in exchange for a higher tuition rate, you get more personal attention. Also, classes are generally smaller, which gives you more opportunity to interact with your professors. And if you want to attend a single-sex school or a school with a religious affiliation, then private school is the only way to go.

big versus small

Do you thrive on getting lost in a crowd or having friends from all different walks of life? Then you most likely won't be happy at a school so small that everyone on campus knows what you had for dinner before you've even removed your tray from the table. A big college provides you with a level of anonymity. And it also offers a variety — in friends, classes, majors, and extracurricular activities. At a large school, you'll have the opportunity to expand your horizons in a way you may have never been able to before, especially if you grew up in a small town. However, what you won't get at a big school is a lot of individual attention. You may wind up with A's in Waiting In Line 101 and Advanced Red Tape. If you're willing to forgo the diversity you'd get at a big school, you'll get a lot more face time with your professors at a smaller college, and you may even get to design your own major. And if you're looking for a school with a strong sense of community, it's pretty easy to find at a small school.

greek versus non-greek

If you've been reciting lines from National Lampoon's *Animal House* since kindergarten or you love the idea of creating an entire wardrobe based on Greek letters, then you're likely to love a college that has a strong Greek fraternity and sorority system. Especially at a large college, having a group of "brothers" or "sisters" can help you develop a real sense of community — not to mention provide you with a calendar full of Friday night mixers. However, schools with strong Greek systems also have reputations for being somewhat elitist and segregated. And if you pride yourself on being a free spirit, you may not be thrilled with the pledge process. Finally, if you're anxious to get away from the social hierarchy of high school cliques, then you may want to think twice before going to a school with a strong Greek system.

competitive versus nurturing

Everyone learns differently. Your motivation for going after that A may be beating out everyone else in the class. Or maybe the only way you can really understand something is by having a teacher talk you through it a couple of times. It's important to choose an environment that works with your learning style. A competitive environment works for those who thrive on a faster pace. However, if fear interferes with your learning rather than motivates you, check out colleges that have the reputation for being more supportive. These are the type of schools where you'll be able to get individualized attention from professors, especially if you're feeling overwhelmed. Also, at schools like this students are more inclined to help one another than to knock each other down to get a better grade. Many of the smaller liberal arts colleges are known for providing a more nurturing environment.

prestige

How important is it that people react with awe and jealousy when you tell them where you go to school? If you aim to impress the country club admission committee, you may want to look into the better-known, prestigious schools.

student body makeup

Are you happiest when surrounded by a cornucopia of colors, religions, and musical tastes? Or do you like to be around people with backgrounds similar to your own? For diversity, check out larger schools.

class offerings

Would it make you happy to know that if you want to take a course on the Symbolism of Water In 16th Century French Art, you could? Or are you more interested in sticking with Psych 101 and classes that pertain to your major? Private schools will have a wider selection of course offerings, whereas public schools tend to stick with the basics.

party schools

Do you plan to minor in Lack of Sleep and major in Advanced Kegging? You will want to check out a big state school or a small private school that has a reputation for being a party school.

activities on campus

Have you met most of your friends through sports or clubs? Then you will want to make sure to check out what each school has to offer in terms of extracurricular activities.

division I and II versus division III schools

You may be a star player on your school's basketball team but still be unable to attract the interest of the coaches of the top college teams. If your love of the sport is greater than your desire to hold out for a coveted spot on one of the more competitive teams, you should look into Division III schools, where you will have a much greater chance of playing. If you are one of the blessed few true all-star athletes and you are looking for a free ride, you will want to apply to and contact coaches at the Division I and II schools, which have the most competitive teams and offer athletic scholarships.

nearby recreation

Do you love rock climbing, hiking, and other outdoor activities? If so, chances are a city school with a concrete campus isn't going to work for you. Conversely, if you prefer to spend your weekends frequenting museums and dining in a different restaurant every night, then a school in the sticks is not going to be a good fit for you.

politics on campus

Is a sit-in or other kind of political demonstration your idea of a perfect first date? Then chances are you'll be happier at a school that's known for its liberal bent. But if you've been a supporter of the GOP since birth, you may be happiest at a college with a more conservative student body.

pre-med/pre-law/business

Already planning to attend Harvard Law, Johns Hopkins Medical, or Wharton Business? You should take a good look at the admissions requirements of your graduate school(s) before deciding where you will go to undergraduate school to make sure you will be able to fulfill all of the requirements.

the arts

Were you born to paint? Are you dying to act? Do you consider yourself nothing without your music? Even if you are not planning to pursue these interests professionally, you will be much happier if you attend a school that has solid course offerings in these areas.

NOTES

HOW TO BUILD YOUR LIST OF COLLEGES

You will find five worksheets at the end of this chapter to help you begin and narrow your search for colleges. If you complete them in order, they will help you build a list of colleges to consider, organize the information you gather about those colleges, narrow down your list of colleges, and ultimately make your final selection of five to eight or so colleges to which you will apply. Do not try to fill these worksheets out all at once. You will need to come back to this section throughout your college search process. Following is the list of worksheets with instructions on how to fill them out.

colleges to research worksheet

This worksheet offers space for more than 30 colleges, so list any school you want to research further. This is a preliminary list, so don't be too picky at this point. You'll find room for only brief notes here. The next worksheet will help you gather more detailed information about each college. This is your springboard into the research process.

college overview worksheet

Once a college has been upgraded from your Colleges to Research worksheet, add to it the College Overview worksheet. The front side of this worksheet will help you determine which category (high-reach, middle-reach, safety) the schools you are interested in fall into. The reverse side of the worksheet will help you determine if the schools listed are good fits for you in other ways. There are ten copies of this worksheet, so you will need to narrow down your list before tackling this worksheet for each college.

In order to fill out the front side of the College Overview worksheet, you will need to have access to a college guidebook or the Internet to find information on school's stats. Visit the college Web site or use a college search engine such as the one provided by the College Board (www.collegeboard.com). Once you do a school search, click on "Admission." Most books and many search engines list a college's acceptable range for SAT and ACT test scores. The numbers usually represent the highest and lowest scores for applicants admitted the previous year. (If you choose the College Board search engine, note that it lists the high and low test scores for the middle 50 percent of applicants.) Record these high and low scores for the college of your choice. In order to fill in your own stats, you will also need to know your GPA and standardized test scores.

Many schools also list the minimum accepted score "for credit" for the AP exams (the minimum required score to receive college credit for a course). Your AP exams are also used for admission evaluations.

Most schools will indicate that they take students up to a certain percentile in their class rank. Although they will not state how many students from each percentile they admit, you should still be able to get a sense of where you fit in the applicant pool. If you know that a school accepts students who fall into the top 30 percent of their class and you are in the top 15 percent of your class, then it is safe to say that as far as academic record is concerned, you are not at the lower end of the applicant pool.

Gather as many statistics as you can when filling out this worksheet, but don't get hung up on filling in every blank. Not all colleges and all sources offer the same stats.

When there is a question of which category a school falls into — high-reach, middle-reach, or safety — go with the weaker category. For example, if a school is a middle-reach for you based on your academic record, but a high-reach based on your standardized test scores, put the school down as a high-reach.

No one wants to think about the possibility that he or she may not be accepted at the college of first choice. But with the ever-increasing competition, it does happen. By taking the time to research and apply to backup schools that you truly find appealing, you will be much happier if one of them turns out to be the place you attend. The best thing you can do for yourself is to be completely realistic about your chances of admission. If you do your research and are completely honest with yourself, there shouldn't be any surprises come April when the colleges send you their decisions.

schools I plan to visit and/or research further worksheet

Colleges that have made it this far on your lists and worksheets should all be good contenders for your final list. This is a good place to check for a reasonable balance of high-reach, middle-reach, and safety schools. Use the notes space here to record information you still need to research or what you hope to learn on a campus visit.

college applicant (and parent) worksheets — redux

Look familiar? This is the same worksheet that you filled out at the beginning of this chapter. Once you have done all (or most) of your research, fill this worksheet out again and compare it to your original to see if your criteria have changed. You should now know a lot more about the options on campuses and what different schools offer. You should have a much clearer idea of what's important to you and what you aren't really concerned about. This information is very valuable because it will help you stay true to what you want in a college and prevent you from getting swept up by someone else's enthusiasm over a school that isn't the right fit for you.

Compare your answers on this worksheet to the attributes of the schools on your College Overview worksheet. Are some schools standing above others? Are there schools you can eliminate because it is now clear they are not good fits for your needs and preferences?

You can use your discretion as to whether or not to ask your parents to fill out their worksheet again. If you think their concerns are going to prevent you from going to the school of your dreams, then asking them to fill out this worksheet again and discuss it with you may be a good way to revisit the topic. However, if this is going to reopen a touchy subject and their concerns do not pertain to the school where you want to apply, then you may want to leave well enough alone.

the final list — where I'm applying to college worksheet

When it comes time to make this final list, you should include a minimum of five schools and no more than eight. To help ensure that you do not wind up with a bunch of thin envelopes come springtime, you should make sure that at least three of the schools on your list are from the combined middle-reach and safety categories. (Obviously, if you apply and are accepted early admission, the five-school minimum does not apply to you. However, if your acceptance is not binding, you may want to go ahead and send in those other applications so you can keep your options open.)

Planning to apply to nine or ten schools or more? It is time to take another pass at your college list before you start filling out applications. If you plan to apply to a college for the sole purpose of seeing whether or not you will be admitted, you should rethink your strategy. First of all, colleges usually have a pretty good idea of those who are serious about their school, based on the effort put forth. So unless you are planning to give 100 percent, you may get rejected based on your lack of interest. Secondly, if you do get accepted, you will be taking a spot away from another student who may have his or her heart set on attending that school. Thirdly, when you factor in the cost involved in submitting applications (upwards of $50 per school), applying to college can get pricey.

Now that you know which colleges you will apply to, you can begin the application process covered in Chapter 4: Applying to College.

COLLEGES TO RESEARCH WORKSHEET

This is your preliminary list of schools, so anything you want to check out online or in a college guide should go on this list. (See page 29 for more detailed instructions on how to complete this worksheet.)

Name ______

Web site ______

NOTES ______

Name ______

Web site ______

NOTES ______

Name ______

Web site ______

NOTES ______

Name ______

Web site ______

NOTES ______

Name ______

Web site ______

NOTES ______

Name ______

Web site ______

NOTES ______

Name ______

Web site ______

NOTES ______

Name ______

Web site ______

NOTES ______

Name ______

Web site ______

NOTES ______

Name ______

Web site ______

NOTES ______

Name ______

Web site ______

NOTES ______

Name ______

Web site ______

NOTES ______

Name ______

Web site ______

NOTES ______

Name ______

Web site ______

NOTES ______

Name ______

Web site ______

NOTES ______

Name ______

Web site ______

NOTES ______

Name ______

Web site ______

NOTES ______

Name ______

Web site ______

NOTES ______

COLLEGES TO RESEARCH WORKSHEET

Name
Web site
NOTES

Name
Web site
NOTES

Name
Web site
NOTES

Name
Web site
NOTES

Name
Web site
NOTES

Name
Web site
NOTES

Name
Web site
NOTES

Name
Web site
NOTES

Name
Web site
NOTES

Name
Web site
NOTES

Name
Web site
NOTES

Name
Web site
NOTES

Name
Web site
NOTES

Name
Web site
NOTES

Name
Web site
NOTES

Name
Web site
NOTES

Name
Web site
NOTES

Name
Web site
NOTES

COLLEGE OVERVIEW WORKSHEET

FOR ______________________
COLLEGE

Using college Web sites and print and online resources, compare the college's high and low stats and percentages to yours to determine if this school is a high-reach, middle-reach, or safety school for you. (See pages 29–30 for more detailed instructions on how to complete both sides of this worksheet.)

test scores

SAT	Verbal	High____	Low____	My Score____
	Math	High____	Low____	My Score____
	Writing	High____	Low____	My Score____
SAT II	____	High____	Low____	My Score____
SAT II	____	High____	Low____	My Score____
SAT II	____	High____	Low____	My Score____
SAT II	____	High____	Low____	My Score____
ACT	English	High____	Low____	My Score____
ACT	Math	High____	Low____	My Score____
ACT	Reading	High____	Low____	My Score____
ACT	Science	High____	Low____	My Score____
ACT	Writing	High____	Low____	My Score____
AP	Composite	High____	Low____	My Score____
AP	____	High____	Low____	My Score____
AP	____	High____	Low____	My Score____
AP	____	High____	Low____	My Score____
AP	____	High____	Low____	My Score____
grade point average		High____	Low____	My GPA____
class rank		Top____	Percentile____	My Rank____

additional attributes *sought by this college*______________________

My attributes______________________

percent of applicants accepted ______%

- ☐ I am in the top 30 percent of applicants
- ☐ I am in the middle 40 percent of applicants
- ☐ I am in the bottom 30 percent of applicants

- ☐ This college is a high-reach choice.
- ☐ This college is a middle-reach choice.
- ☐ This college is a safety choice.
- ☐ I am not going to apply to this college.

- ☐ The tuition ($__________ per year) is a consideration.
- ☐ The location (______________) is a consideration.
- ☐ Other: ______________ is a consideration.

Notes

____

FOR ______________________________ COLLEGE

The academic environment at this college is ______________________________

This ☐ **is** ☐ **isn't** a good fit for me because ______________________________

On a scale of 1–5, how important is this? (circle one) 1 2 3 4 5

The extracurricular activities at this college include ______________________________

This ☐ **is** ☐ **isn't** a good fit for me because ______________________________

On a scale of 1–5, how important is this? (circle one) 1 2 3 4 5

This college is located in ______________ *(the city, the suburbs, a college town, the country)*

This ☐ **is** ☐ **isn't** a good fit for me because ______________________________

On a scale of 1–5, how important is this? (circle one) 1 2 3 4 5

This college is located in the ______________ *region of the country.*

This ☐ **is** ☐ **isn't** a good fit for me because ______________________________

On a scale of 1–5, how important is this? (circle one) 1 2 3 4 5

The size of this college is ______________

This ☐ **is** ☐ **isn't** a good fit for me because ______________________________

On a scale of 1–5, how important is this? (circle one) 1 2 3 4 5

The social scene consists mostly of ______________________________

This ☐ **is** ☐ **isn't** a good fit for me because ______________________________

On a scale of 1–5, how important is this? (circle one) 1 2 3 4 5

Most students like to (culture, leisure) ______________________________

This ☐ **is** ☐ **isn't** a good fit for me because ______________________________

On a scale of 1–5, how important is this? (circle one) 1 2 3 4 5

Outdoor recreational activities for students at this college include ______________________________

This ☐ **is** ☐ **isn't** a good fit for me because ______________________________

On a scale of 1–5, how important is this? (circle one) 1 2 3 4 5

Politically, most of the students at this college are ______________________________

This ☐ **is** ☐ **isn't** a good fit for me because ______________________________

On a scale of 1–5, how important is this? (circle one) 1 2 3 4 5

Most of the students at this college are from ______________________________

This ☐ **is** ☐ **isn't** a good fit for me because ______________________________

On a scale of 1–5, how important is this? (circle one) 1 2 3 4 5

The weather in this region is ______________________________

This ☐ **is** ☐ **isn't** a good fit for me because ______________________________

On a scale of 1–5, how important is this? (circle one) 1 2 3 4 5

The distance from my family's home to this college is ______________

This ☐ **is** ☐ **isn't** a good fit for me because ______________________________

On a scale of 1–5, how important is this? (circle one) 1 2 3 4 5

The tuition at this college is ______________

This ☐ **is** ☐ **isn't** a good fit for me because ______________________________

On a scale of 1–5, how important is this? (circle one) 1 2 3 4 5

☐ **will** ☐ **won't** need financial aid.

This ☐ **is** ☐ **isn't** a good fit for me because ______________________________

On a scale of 1–5, how important is this? (circle one) 1 2 3 4 5

My three favorite things about this college are

1. ______________
2. ______________
3. ______________

My three least favorite things about this college are

1. ______________
2. ______________
3. ______________

COLLEGE OVERVIEW WORKSHEET

FOR ______________________
COLLEGE

Using college Web sites and print and online resources, compare the college's high and low stats and percentages to yours to determine if this school is a high-reach, middle-reach, or safety school for you. (See pages 29–30 for more detailed instructions on how to complete both sides of this worksheet.)

test scores

SAT	Verbal	High____	Low____	My Score____
	Math	High____	Low____	My Score____
	Writing	High____	Low____	My Score____
SAT II	____	High____	Low____	My Score____
SAT II	____	High____	Low____	My Score____
SAT II	____	High____	Low____	My Score____
SAT II	____	High____	Low____	My Score____
ACT	English	High____	Low____	My Score____
ACT	Math	High____	Low____	My Score____
ACT	Reading	High____	Low____	My Score____
ACT	Science	High____	Low____	My Score____
ACT	Writing	High____	Low____	My Score____
AP	Composite	High____	Low____	My Score____
AP	____	High____	Low____	My Score____
AP	____	High____	Low____	My Score____
AP	____	High____	Low____	My Score____
AP	____	High____	Low____	My Score____

grade point average
High____ Low____ My GPA____

class rank
Top____ Percentile____ My Rank____

additional attributes *sought by this college*____

My attributes____

percent of applicants accepted ____%

- ☐ I am in the top 30 percent of applicants
- ☐ I am in the middle 40 percent of applicants
- ☐ I am in the bottom 30 percent of applicants

- ☐ This college is a high-reach choice.
- ☐ This college is a middle-reach choice.
- ☐ This college is a safety choice.
- ☐ I am not going to apply to this college.

- ☐ The tuition ($____ per year) is a consideration.
- ☐ The location (____) is a consideration.
- ☐ Other: ____ is a consideration.

NOTES

FOR ____________________

COLLEGE

The academic environment at this college is ____________________

This ☐ **is** ☐ **isn't** a good fit for me because ____________________

On a scale of 1–5, how important is this?
(circle one) 1 2 3 4 5

The extracurricular activities at this college include ____________________

This ☐ **is** ☐ **isn't** a good fit for me because ____________________

On a scale of 1–5, how important is this?
(circle one) 1 2 3 4 5

This college is located in ____________________ *(the city, the suburbs, a college town, the country)*

This ☐ **is** ☐ **isn't** a good fit for me because ____________________

On a scale of 1–5, how important is this?
(circle one) 1 2 3 4 5

This college is located in the ____________ *region of the country.*

This ☐ **is** ☐ **isn't** a good fit for me because ____________________

On a scale of 1–5, how important is this?
(circle one) 1 2 3 4 5

The size of this college is ____________________

This ☐ **is** ☐ **isn't** a good fit for me because ____________________

On a scale of 1–5, how important is this?
(circle one) 1 2 3 4 5

The social scene consists mostly of ____________________

This ☐ **is** ☐ **isn't** a good fit for me because ____________________

On a scale of 1–5, how important is this?
(circle one) 1 2 3 4 5

Most students like to (culture, leisure) ____________________

This ☐ **is** ☐ **isn't** a good fit for me because ____________________

On a scale of 1–5, how important is this?
(circle one) 1 2 3 4 5

Outdoor recreational activities for students at this college include ____________________

This ☐ **is** ☐ **isn't** a good fit for me because ____________________

On a scale of 1–5, how important is this?
(circle one) 1 2 3 4 5

Politically, most of the students at this college are ____________________

This ☐ **is** ☐ **isn't** a good fit for me because ____________________

On a scale of 1–5, how important is this?
(circle one) 1 2 3 4 5

Most of the students at this college are from ____________________

This ☐ **is** ☐ **isn't** a good fit for me because ____________________

On a scale of 1–5, how important is this?
(circle one) 1 2 3 4 5

The weather in this region is ____________________

This ☐ **is** ☐ **isn't** a good fit for me because ____________________

On a scale of 1–5, how important is this?
(circle one) 1 2 3 4 5

The distance from my family's home to this college is ____________________

This ☐ **is** ☐ **isn't** a good fit for me because ____________________

On a scale of 1–5, how important is this?
(circle one) 1 2 3 4 5

The tuition at this college is ____________________

This ☐ **is** ☐ **isn't** a good fit for me because ____________________

On a scale of 1–5, how important is this?
(circle one) 1 2 3 4 5

☐ **will** ☐ **won't** need financial aid.

This ☐ **is** ☐ **isn't** a good fit for me because ____________________

On a scale of 1–5, how important is this?
(circle one) 1 2 3 4 5

My three favorite things about this college are

1. ____________________
2. ____________________
3. ____________________

My three least favorite things about this college are

1. ____________________
2. ____________________
3. ____________________

COLLEGE OVERVIEW WORKSHEET

FOR ______________________ **COLLEGE**

Using college Web sites and print and online resources, compare the college's high and low stats and percentages to yours to determine if this school is a high-reach, middle-reach, or safety school for you. (See pages 29–30 for more detailed instructions on how to complete both sides of this worksheet.)

test scores

SAT	Verbal	High ____	Low ____	My Score ____
	Math	High ____	Low ____	My Score ____
	Writing	High ____	Low ____	My Score ____
SAT II	____	High ____	Low ____	My Score ____
SAT II	____	High ____	Low ____	My Score ____
SAT II	____	High ____	Low ____	My Score ____
SAT II	____	High ____	Low ____	My Score ____
ACT	English	High ____	Low ____	My Score ____
ACT	Math	High ____	Low ____	My Score ____
ACT	Reading	High ____	Low ____	My Score ____
ACT	Science	High ____	Low ____	My Score ____
ACT	Writing	High ____	Low ____	My Score ____
AP	Composite	High ____	Low ____	My Score ____
AP	____	High ____	Low ____	My Score ____
AP	____	High ____	Low ____	My Score ____
AP	____	High ____	Low ____	My Score ____
AP	____	High ____	Low ____	My Score ____
grade point average		High ____	Low ____	My GPA ____
class rank		Top ____	Percentile ____	My Rank ____

additional attributes *sought by this college* ______________________

My attributes ______________________

percent of applicants accepted ____ %

- ☐ I am in the top 30 percent of applicants
- ☐ I am in the middle 40 percent of applicants
- ☐ I am in the bottom 30 percent of applicants

- ☐ This college is a high-reach choice.
- ☐ This college is a middle-reach choice.
- ☐ This college is a safety choice.
- ☐ I am not going to apply to this college.

- ☐ The tuition ($ ____ per year) is a consideration.
- ☐ The location (____) is a consideration.
- ☐ Other: ____ is a consideration.

NOTES

____

FOR ______________________________

COLLEGE

The academic environment at this college is ______________________________

____

This ☐ **is** ☐ **isn't** a good fit for me because ______________________________

On a scale of 1–5, how important is this?
(circle one) 1 2 3 4 5

The extracurricular activities at this college include ______________________________

____

This ☐ **is** ☐ **isn't** a good fit for me because ______________________________

On a scale of 1–5, how important is this?
(circle one) 1 2 3 4 5

This college is located in ______________ *(the city, the suburbs, a college town, the country)*

This ☐ **is** ☐ **isn't** a good fit for me because ______________________________

On a scale of 1–5, how important is this?
(circle one) 1 2 3 4 5

This college is located in the ______________ *region of the country.*

This ☐ **is** ☐ **isn't** a good fit for me because ______________________________

On a scale of 1–5, how important is this?
(circle one) 1 2 3 4 5

The size of this college is ______________

This ☐ **is** ☐ **isn't** a good fit for me because ______________________________

On a scale of 1–5, how important is this?
(circle one) 1 2 3 4 5

The social scene consists mostly of ______________________________

____

____

This ☐ **is** ☐ **isn't** a good fit for me because ______________________________

On a scale of 1–5, how important is this?
(circle one) 1 2 3 4 5

Most students like to (culture, leisure) ______________________________

____

____

This ☐ **is** ☐ **isn't** a good fit for me because ______________________________

On a scale of 1–5, how important is this?
(circle one) 1 2 3 4 5

Outdoor recreational activities for students at this college include ______________________________

____

____

This ☐ **is** ☐ **isn't** a good fit for me because ______________________________

On a scale of 1–5, how important is this?
(circle one) 1 2 3 4 5

Politically, most of the students at this college are ______________________________

____

This ☐ **is** ☐ **isn't** a good fit for me because ______________________________

On a scale of 1–5, how important is this?
(circle one) 1 2 3 4 5

Most of the students at this college are from ______________________________

____

This ☐ **is** ☐ **isn't** a good fit for me because ______________________________

On a scale of 1–5, how important is this?
(circle one) 1 2 3 4 5

The weather in this region is ______________________________

____

____

This ☐ **is** ☐ **isn't** a good fit for me because ______________________________

On a scale of 1–5, how important is this?
(circle one) 1 2 3 4 5

The distance from my family's home to this college is ______________________________

This ☐ **is** ☐ **isn't** a good fit for me because ______________________________

On a scale of 1–5, how important is this?
(circle one) 1 2 3 4 5

The tuition at this college is ______________

This ☐ **is** ☐ **isn't** a good fit for me because ______________________________

On a scale of 1–5, how important is this?
(circle one) 1 2 3 4 5

☐ **will** ☐ **won't** need financial aid.

This ☐ **is** ☐ **isn't** a good fit for me because ______________________________

On a scale of 1–5, how important is this?
(circle one) 1 2 3 4 5

My three favorite things about this college are

1. ______________________________
2. ______________________________
3. ______________________________

My three least favorite things about this college are

1. ______________________________
2. ______________________________
3. ______________________________

COLLEGE OVERVIEW WORKSHEET

FOR ______________________
COLLEGE

Using college Web sites and print and online resources, compare the college's high and low stats and percentages to yours to determine if this school is a high-reach, middle-reach, or safety school for you. (See pages 29–30 for more detailed instructions on how to complete both sides of this worksheet.)

test scores

SAT	Verbal	High______	Low______	My Score______
	Math	High______	Low______	My Score______
	Writing	High______	Low______	My Score______
SAT II	______	High______	Low______	My Score______
SAT II	______	High______	Low______	My Score______
SAT II	______	High______	Low______	My Score______
SAT II	______	High______	Low______	My Score______
ACT	English	High______	Low______	My Score______
ACT	Math	High______	Low______	My Score______
ACT	Reading	High______	Low______	My Score______
ACT	Science	High______	Low______	My Score______
ACT	Writing	High______	Low______	My Score______
AP	Composite	High______	Low______	My Score______
AP	______	High______	Low______	My Score______
AP	______	High______	Low______	My Score______
AP	______	High______	Low______	My Score______
AP	______	High______	Low______	My Score______

grade point average High______ Low______ My GPA______

class rank Top______ Percentile______ My Rank______

additional attributes *sought by this college* ______________________

My attributes ______________________

percent of applicants accepted ______%

- ☐ I am in the top 30 percent of applicants
- ☐ I am in the middle 40 percent of applicants
- ☐ I am in the bottom 30 percent of applicants

- ☐ This college is a high-reach choice.
- ☐ This college is a middle-reach choice.
- ☐ This college is a safety choice.
- ☐ I am not going to apply to this college.

- ☐ The tuition ($__________ per year) is a consideration.
- ☐ The location (______________) is a consideration.
- ☐ Other: __________ is a consideration.

NOTES

____

FOR ______________________________ COLLEGE

The academic environment at this college is ______________________________

This ☐ **is** ☐ **isn't** a good fit for me because ______________________________

On a scale of 1–5, how important is this?
(circle one) 1 2 3 4 5

The extracurricular activities at this college include ______________________________

This ☐ **is** ☐ **isn't** a good fit for me because ______________________________

On a scale of 1–5, how important is this?
(circle one) 1 2 3 4 5

This college is located in ______________ *(the city, the suburbs, a college town, the country)*

This ☐ **is** ☐ **isn't** a good fit for me because ______________________________

On a scale of 1–5, how important is this?
(circle one) 1 2 3 4 5

This college is located in the ______________ *region of the country.*

This ☐ **is** ☐ **isn't** a good fit for me because ______________________________

On a scale of 1–5, how important is this?
(circle one) 1 2 3 4 5

The size of this college is ______________

This ☐ **is** ☐ **isn't** a good fit for me because ______________________________

On a scale of 1–5, how important is this?
(circle one) 1 2 3 4 5

The social scene consists mostly of ______________________________

This ☐ **is** ☐ **isn't** a good fit for me because ______________________________

On a scale of 1–5, how important is this?
(circle one) 1 2 3 4 5

Most students like to (culture, leisure) ______________________________

This ☐ **is** ☐ **isn't** a good fit for me because ______________________________

On a scale of 1–5, how important is this?
(circle one) 1 2 3 4 5

Outdoor recreational activities for students at this college include ______________________________

This ☐ **is** ☐ **isn't** a good fit for me because ______________________________

On a scale of 1–5, how important is this?
(circle one) 1 2 3 4 5

Politically, most of the students at this college are ______________________________

This ☐ **is** ☐ **isn't** a good fit for me because ______________________________

On a scale of 1–5, how important is this?
(circle one) 1 2 3 4 5

Most of the students at this college are from ______________________________

This ☐ **is** ☐ **isn't** a good fit for me because ______________________________

On a scale of 1–5, how important is this?
(circle one) 1 2 3 4 5

The weather in this region is ______________________________

This ☐ **is** ☐ **isn't** a good fit for me because ______________________________

On a scale of 1–5, how important is this?
(circle one) 1 2 3 4 5

The distance from my family's home to this college is ______________

This ☐ **is** ☐ **isn't** a good fit for me because ______________________________

On a scale of 1–5, how important is this?
(circle one) 1 2 3 4 5

The tuition at this college is ______________

This ☐ **is** ☐ **isn't** a good fit for me because ______________________________

On a scale of 1–5, how important is this?
(circle one) 1 2 3 4 5

☐ **will** ☐ **won't** need financial aid.

This ☐ **is** ☐ **isn't** a good fit for me because ______________________________

On a scale of 1–5, how important is this?
(circle one) 1 2 3 4 5

My three favorite things about this college are

1. ______________
2. ______________
3. ______________

My three least favorite things about this college are

1. ______________
2. ______________
3. ______________

COLLEGE OVERVIEW WORKSHEET

FOR ______________________ COLLEGE

Using college Web sites and print and online resources, compare the college's high and low stats and percentages to yours to determine if this school is a high-reach, middle-reach, or safety school for you. (See pages 29–30 for more detailed instructions on how to complete both sides of this worksheet.)

test scores

SAT	Verbal	High ______	Low ______	My Score ______
	Math	High ______	Low ______	My Score ______
	Writing	High ______	Low ______	My Score ______
SAT II	______	High ______	Low ______	My Score ______
SAT II	______	High ______	Low ______	My Score ______
SAT II	______	High ______	Low ______	My Score ______
SAT II	______	High ______	Low ______	My Score ______
ACT	English	High ______	Low ______	My Score ______
ACT	Math	High ______	Low ______	My Score ______
ACT	Reading	High ______	Low ______	My Score ______
ACT	Science	High ______	Low ______	My Score ______
ACT	Writing	High ______	Low ______	My Score ______
AP	Composite	High ______	Low ______	My Score ______
AP	______	High ______	Low ______	My Score ______
AP	______	High ______	Low ______	My Score ______
AP	______	High ______	Low ______	My Score ______
AP	______	High ______	Low ______	My Score ______

grade point average High ______ Low ______ My GPA ______

class rank Top ______ Percentile ______ My Rank ______

additional attributes *sought by this college* ______________________

My attributes ______________________

percent of applicants accepted ______ %

- ☐ I am in the top 30 percent of applicants
- ☐ I am in the middle 40 percent of applicants
- ☐ I am in the bottom 30 percent of applicants

- ☐ This college is a high-reach choice.
- ☐ This college is a middle-reach choice.
- ☐ This college is a safety choice.
- ☐ I am not going to apply to this college.

- ☐ The tuition ($______ per year) is a consideration.
- ☐ The location (______________) is a consideration.
- ☐ Other: ______________ is a consideration.

NOTES

____

FOR ______________________________

COLLEGE

The academic environment at this college is ______________________________

____

This ☐ **is** ☐ **isn't** a good fit for me because

____

On a scale of 1–5, how important is this?
(circle one) 1 2 3 4 5

The extracurricular activities at this college include ______________________________

____

This ☐ **is** ☐ **isn't** a good fit for me because

____

On a scale of 1–5, how important is this?
(circle one) 1 2 3 4 5

This college is located in ______________________________
(the city, the suburbs, a college town, the country)

This ☐ **is** ☐ **isn't** a good fit for me because

____

On a scale of 1–5, how important is this?
(circle one) 1 2 3 4 5

This college is located in the ______________ *region of the country.*

This ☐ **is** ☐ **isn't** a good fit for me because

____

On a scale of 1–5, how important is this?
(circle one) 1 2 3 4 5

The size of this college is ______________________________

This ☐ **is** ☐ **isn't** a good fit for me because

____

On a scale of 1–5, how important is this?
(circle one) 1 2 3 4 5

The social scene consists mostly of ______________________________

____

____

This ☐ **is** ☐ **isn't** a good fit for me because

____

On a scale of 1–5, how important is this?
(circle one) 1 2 3 4 5

Most students like to (culture, leisure) ______________________________

____

____

This ☐ **is** ☐ **isn't** a good fit for me because

____

On a scale of 1–5, how important is this?
(circle one) 1 2 3 4 5

Outdoor recreational activities for students at this college include ______________________________

____

____

This ☐ **is** ☐ **isn't** a good fit for me because

____

On a scale of 1–5, how important is this?
(circle one) 1 2 3 4 5

Politically, most of the students at this college are ______________________________

____

This ☐ **is** ☐ **isn't** a good fit for me because

____

On a scale of 1–5, how important is this?
(circle one) 1 2 3 4 5

Most of the students at this college are from ______________________________

____

This ☐ **is** ☐ **isn't** a good fit for me because

____

On a scale of 1–5, how important is this?
(circle one) 1 2 3 4 5

The weather in this region is ______________________________

____

____

This ☐ **is** ☐ **isn't** a good fit for me because

____

On a scale of 1–5, how important is this?
(circle one) 1 2 3 4 5

The distance from my family's home to this college is ______________________________

This ☐ **is** ☐ **isn't** a good fit for me because

____

On a scale of 1–5, how important is this?
(circle one) 1 2 3 4 5

The tuition at this college is ______________________________

This ☐ **is** ☐ **isn't** a good fit for me because

____

On a scale of 1–5, how important is this?
(circle one) 1 2 3 4 5

☐ **will** ☐ **won't** need financial aid.

This ☐ **is** ☐ **isn't** a good fit for me because

____

On a scale of 1–5, how important is this?
(circle one) 1 2 3 4 5

My three favorite things about this college are

1. ______________________________
2. ______________________________
3. ______________________________

My three least favorite things about this college are

1. ______________________________
2. ______________________________
3. ______________________________

COLLEGE OVERVIEW WORKSHEET

FOR ______________________
COLLEGE

Using college Web sites and print and online resources, compare the college's high and low stats and percentages to yours to determine if this school is a high-reach, middle-reach, or safety school for you. (See pages 29–30 for more detailed instructions on how to complete both sides of this worksheet.)

test scores

SAT	Verbal	High______	Low______	My Score______
	Math	High______	Low______	My Score______
	Writing	High______	Low______	My Score______
SAT II	______	High______	Low______	My Score______
SAT II	______	High______	Low______	My Score______
SAT II	______	High______	Low______	My Score______
SAT II	______	High______	Low______	My Score______
ACT	English	High______	Low______	My Score______
ACT	Math	High______	Low______	My Score______
ACT	Reading	High______	Low______	My Score______
ACT	Science	High______	Low______	My Score______
ACT	Writing	High______	Low______	My Score______
AP	Composite	High______	Low______	My Score______
AP	______	High______	Low______	My Score______
AP	______	High______	Low______	My Score______
AP	______	High______	Low______	My Score______
AP	______	High______	Low______	My Score______

grade point average High______ Low______ My GPA______

class rank Top______ Percentile______ My Rank______

additional attributes *sought by this college* ______________________

My attributes ______________________

percent of applicants accepted ______%

- ☐ I am in the top 30 percent of applicants
- ☐ I am in the middle 40 percent of applicants
- ☐ I am in the bottom 30 percent of applicants

- ☐ This college is a high-reach choice.
- ☐ This college is a middle-reach choice.
- ☐ This college is a safety choice.
- ☐ I am not going to apply to this college.

- ☐ The tuition ($______ per year) is a consideration.
- ☐ The location (______________) is a consideration.
- ☐ Other: ______________ is a consideration.

NOTES

FOR ______________________________

COLLEGE

The academic environment at this college is ______________________________

____

This ☐ **is** ☐ **isn't** a good fit for me because

____

On a scale of 1–5, how important is this?
(circle one) 1 2 3 4 5

The extracurricular activities at this college include ______________________________

____

This ☐ **is** ☐ **isn't** a good fit for me because

____

On a scale of 1–5, how important is this?
(circle one) 1 2 3 4 5

This college is located in ______________________________ *(the city, the suburbs, a college town, the country)*

This ☐ **is** ☐ **isn't** a good fit for me because

____

On a scale of 1–5, how important is this?
(circle one) 1 2 3 4 5

This college is located in the ______________________________ *region of the country.*

This ☐ **is** ☐ **isn't** a good fit for me because

____

On a scale of 1–5, how important is this?
(circle one) 1 2 3 4 5

The size of this college is ______________________________

This ☐ **is** ☐ **isn't** a good fit for me because

____

On a scale of 1–5, how important is this?
(circle one) 1 2 3 4 5

The social scene consists mostly of ______________________________

____

____

This ☐ **is** ☐ **isn't** a good fit for me because

____

On a scale of 1–5, how important is this?
(circle one) 1 2 3 4 5

Most students like to (culture, leisure) ______________________________

____

____

This ☐ **is** ☐ **isn't** a good fit for me because

____

On a scale of 1–5, how important is this?
(circle one) 1 2 3 4 5

Outdoor recreational activities for students at this college include ______________________________

____

____

This ☐ **is** ☐ **isn't** a good fit for me because

____

On a scale of 1–5, how important is this?
(circle one) 1 2 3 4 5

Politically, most of the students at this college are ______________________________

____

This ☐ **is** ☐ **isn't** a good fit for me because

____

On a scale of 1–5, how important is this?
(circle one) 1 2 3 4 5

Most of the students at this college are from ______________________________

____

This ☐ **is** ☐ **isn't** a good fit for me because

____

On a scale of 1–5, how important is this?
(circle one) 1 2 3 4 5

The weather in this region is ______________________________

____

____

This ☐ **is** ☐ **isn't** a good fit for me because

____

On a scale of 1–5, how important is this?
(circle one) 1 2 3 4 5

The distance from my family's home to this college is ______________________________

This ☐ **is** ☐ **isn't** a good fit for me because

____

On a scale of 1–5, how important is this?
(circle one) 1 2 3 4 5

The tuition at this college is ______________________________

This ☐ **is** ☐ **isn't** a good fit for me because

____

On a scale of 1–5, how important is this?
(circle one) 1 2 3 4 5

☐ **will** ☐ **won't** need financial aid.

This ☐ **is** ☐ **isn't** a good fit for me because

____

On a scale of 1–5, how important is this?
(circle one) 1 2 3 4 5

My three favorite things about this college are

1. ______________________________
2. ______________________________
3. ______________________________

My three least favorite things about this college are

1. ______________________________
2. ______________________________
3. ______________________________

COLLEGE OVERVIEW WORKSHEET

FOR ______________________
COLLEGE

Using college Web sites and print and online resources, compare the college's high and low stats and percentages to yours to determine if this school is a high-reach, middle-reach, or safety school for you. (See pages 29–30 for more detailed instructions on how to complete both sides of this worksheet.)

test scores

SAT	Verbal	High______	Low______	My Score______
	Math	High______	Low______	My Score______
	Writing	High______	Low______	My Score______
SAT II	______	High______	Low______	My Score______
SAT II	______	High______	Low______	My Score______
SAT II	______	High______	Low______	My Score______
SAT II	______	High______	Low______	My Score______
ACT	English	High______	Low______	My Score______
ACT	Math	High______	Low______	My Score______
ACT	Reading	High______	Low______	My Score______
ACT	Science	High______	Low______	My Score______
ACT	Writing	High______	Low______	My Score______
AP	Composite	High______	Low______	My Score______
AP	______	High______	Low______	My Score______
AP	______	High______	Low______	My Score______
AP	______	High______	Low______	My Score______
AP	______	High______	Low______	My Score______

grade point average High______ Low______ My GPA______

class rank Top______ Percentile______ My Rank______

additional attributes *sought by this college* ______________________

My attributes ______________________

percent of applicants accepted ______%

- ☐ I am in the top 30 percent of applicants
- ☐ I am in the middle 40 percent of applicants
- ☐ I am in the bottom 30 percent of applicants

- ☐ This college is a high-reach choice.
- ☐ This college is a safety choice.
- ☐ This college is a middle-reach choice.
- ☐ I am not going to apply to this college.

- ☐ The tuition ($______ per year) is a consideration.
- ☐ The location (______) is a consideration.
- ☐ Other: ______ is a consideration.

NOTES

FOR ____________________

COLLEGE

The academic environment at this college is ____________________

This ☐ **is** ☐ **isn't** a good fit for me because ____________________

On a scale of 1–5, how important is this? (circle one) 1 2 3 4 5

The extracurricular activities at this college include ____________________

This ☐ **is** ☐ **isn't** a good fit for me because ____________________

On a scale of 1–5, how important is this? (circle one) 1 2 3 4 5

This college is located in ____________________ *(the city, the suburbs, a college town, the country)*

This ☐ **is** ☐ **isn't** a good fit for me because ____________________

On a scale of 1–5, how important is this? (circle one) 1 2 3 4 5

This college is located in the ____________________ *region of the country.*

This ☐ **is** ☐ **isn't** a good fit for me because ____________________

On a scale of 1–5, how important is this? (circle one) 1 2 3 4 5

The size of this college is ____________________

This ☐ **is** ☐ **isn't** a good fit for me because ____________________

On a scale of 1–5, how important is this? (circle one) 1 2 3 4 5

The social scene consists mostly of ____________________

This ☐ **is** ☐ **isn't** a good fit for me because ____________________

On a scale of 1–5, how important is this? (circle one) 1 2 3 4 5

Most students like to (culture, leisure) ____________________

This ☐ **is** ☐ **isn't** a good fit for me because ____________________

On a scale of 1–5, how important is this? (circle one) 1 2 3 4 5

Outdoor recreational activities for students at this college include ____________________

This ☐ **is** ☐ **isn't** a good fit for me because ____________________

On a scale of 1–5, how important is this? (circle one) 1 2 3 4 5

Politically, most of the students at this college are ____________________

This ☐ **is** ☐ **isn't** a good fit for me because ____________________

On a scale of 1–5, how important is this? (circle one) 1 2 3 4 5

Most of the students at this college are from ____________________

This ☐ **is** ☐ **isn't** a good fit for me because ____________________

On a scale of 1–5, how important is this? (circle one) 1 2 3 4 5

The weather in this region is ____________________

This ☐ **is** ☐ **isn't** a good fit for me because ____________________

On a scale of 1–5, how important is this? (circle one) 1 2 3 4 5

The distance from my family's home to this college is ____________________

This ☐ **is** ☐ **isn't** a good fit for me because ____________________

On a scale of 1–5, how important is this? (circle one) 1 2 3 4 5

The tuition at this college is ____________________

This ☐ **is** ☐ **isn't** a good fit for me because ____________________

On a scale of 1–5, how important is this? (circle one) 1 2 3 4 5

☐ **will** ☐ **won't** need financial aid.

This ☐ **is** ☐ **isn't** a good fit for me because ____________________

On a scale of 1–5, how important is this? (circle one) 1 2 3 4 5

My three favorite things about this college are

1. ____________________
2. ____________________
3. ____________________

My three least favorite things about this college are

1. ____________________
2. ____________________
3. ____________________

COLLEGE OVERVIEW WORKSHEET

FOR ______________________
COLLEGE

Using college Web sites and print and online resources, compare the college's high and low stats and percentages to yours to determine if this school is a high-reach, middle-reach, or safety school for you. (See pages 29–30 for more detailed instructions on how to complete both sides of this worksheet.)

test scores

SAT	Verbal	High____	Low____	My Score____
	Math	High____	Low____	My Score____
	Writing	High____	Low____	My Score____
SAT II	____	High____	Low____	My Score____
SAT II	____	High____	Low____	My Score____
SAT II	____	High____	Low____	My Score____
SAT II	____	High____	Low____	My Score____
ACT	English	High____	Low____	My Score____
ACT	Math	High____	Low____	My Score____
ACT	Reading	High____	Low____	My Score____
ACT	Science	High____	Low____	My Score____
ACT	Writing	High____	Low____	My Score____
AP	Composite	High____	Low____	My Score____
AP	____	High____	Low____	My Score____
AP	____	High____	Low____	My Score____
AP	____	High____	Low____	My Score____
AP	____	High____	Low____	My Score____
grade point average		High____	Low____	My GPA____
class rank		Top____	Percentile____	My Rank____

additional attributes *sought by this college* ______________________

My attributes ______________________

percent of applicants accepted ______%

☐ I am in the top 30 percent of applicants

☐ I am in the middle 40 percent of applicants

☐ I am in the bottom 30 percent of applicants

☐ This college is a high-reach choice.

☐ This college is a middle-reach choice.

☐ This college is a safety choice.

☐ I am not going to apply to this college.

☐ The tuition ($__________ per year) is a consideration.

☐ The location (__________) is a consideration.

☐ Other: __________ is a consideration.

NOTES

FOR ______________________________
COLLEGE

The academic environment at this college is ______________________________

This ☐ **is** ☐ **isn't** a good fit for me because ______________________________

On a scale of 1–5, how important is this?
(circle one) 1 2 3 4 5

The extracurricular activities at this college include ______________________________

This ☐ **is** ☐ **isn't** a good fit for me because ______________________________

On a scale of 1–5, how important is this?
(circle one) 1 2 3 4 5

This college is located in ______________ *(the city, the suburbs, a college town, the country)*

This ☐ **is** ☐ **isn't** a good fit for me because ______________________________

On a scale of 1–5, how important is this?
(circle one) 1 2 3 4 5

This college is located in the ______________ *region of the country.*

This ☐ **is** ☐ **isn't** a good fit for me because ______________________________

On a scale of 1–5, how important is this?
(circle one) 1 2 3 4 5

The size of this college is ______________

This ☐ **is** ☐ **isn't** a good fit for me because ______________________________

On a scale of 1–5, how important is this?
(circle one) 1 2 3 4 5

The social scene consists mostly of ______________________________

This ☐ **is** ☐ **isn't** a good fit for me because ______________________________

On a scale of 1–5, how important is this?
(circle one) 1 2 3 4 5

Most students like to (culture, leisure) ______________________________

This ☐ **is** ☐ **isn't** a good fit for me because ______________________________

On a scale of 1–5, how important is this?
(circle one) 1 2 3 4 5

Outdoor recreational activities for students at this college include ______________________________

This ☐ **is** ☐ **isn't** a good fit for me because ______________________________

On a scale of 1–5, how important is this?
(circle one) 1 2 3 4 5

Politically, most of the students at this college are ______________________________

This ☐ **is** ☐ **isn't** a good fit for me because ______________________________

On a scale of 1–5, how important is this?
(circle one) 1 2 3 4 5

Most of the students at this college are from ______________________________

This ☐ **is** ☐ **isn't** a good fit for me because ______________________________

On a scale of 1–5, how important is this?
(circle one) 1 2 3 4 5

The weather in this region is ______________________________

This ☐ **is** ☐ **isn't** a good fit for me because ______________________________

On a scale of 1–5, how important is this?
(circle one) 1 2 3 4 5

The distance from my family's home to this college is ______________

This ☐ **is** ☐ **isn't** a good fit for me because ______________________________

On a scale of 1–5, how important is this?
(circle one) 1 2 3 4 5

The tuition at this college is ______________

This ☐ **is** ☐ **isn't** a good fit for me because ______________________________

On a scale of 1–5, how important is this?
(circle one) 1 2 3 4 5

☐ **will** ☐ **won't** need financial aid.

This ☐ **is** ☐ **isn't** a good fit for me because ______________________________

On a scale of 1–5, how important is this?
(circle one) 1 2 3 4 5

My three favorite things about this college are

1. ______________
2. ______________
3. ______________

My three least favorite things about this college are

1. ______________
2. ______________
3. ______________

COLLEGE OVERVIEW WORKSHEET

FOR ______________________
COLLEGE

Using college Web sites and print and online resources, compare the college's high and low stats and percentages to yours to determine if this school is a high-reach, middle-reach, or safety school for you. (See pages 29–30 for more detailed instructions on how to complete both sides of this worksheet.)

test scores

SAT	Verbal	High____	Low____	My Score____
	Math	High____	Low____	My Score____
	Writing	High____	Low____	My Score____
SAT II	____	High____	Low____	My Score____
SAT II	____	High____	Low____	My Score____
SAT II	____	High____	Low____	My Score____
SAT II	____	High____	Low____	My Score____
ACT	English	High____	Low____	My Score____
ACT	Math	High____	Low____	My Score____
ACT	Reading	High____	Low____	My Score____
ACT	Science	High____	Low____	My Score____
ACT	Writing	High____	Low____	My Score____
AP	Composite	High____	Low____	My Score____
AP	____	High____	Low____	My Score____
AP	____	High____	Low____	My Score____
AP	____	High____	Low____	My Score____
AP	____	High____	Low____	My Score____
grade point average		High____	Low____	My GPA____
class rank		Top____	Percentile____	My Rank____

additional attributes *sought by this college* ______________________

My attributes ______________________

percent of applicants accepted ______%

- ☐ I am in the top 30 percent of applicants
- ☐ I am in the middle 40 percent of applicants
- ☐ I am in the bottom 30 percent of applicants

- ☐ This college is a high-reach choice.
- ☐ This college is a middle-reach choice.
- ☐ This college is a safety choice.
- ☐ I am not going to apply to this college.

- ☐ The tuition ($__________ per year) is a consideration.
- ☐ The location (______________) is a consideration.
- ☐ Other: __________ is a consideration.

NOTES

FOR ______________________________

COLLEGE

The academic environment at this college is ______________________________

This ☐ **is** ☐ **isn't** a good fit for me because ______________________________

On a scale of 1–5, how important is this?
(circle one) 1 2 3 4 5

The extracurricular activities at this college include ______________________________

This ☐ **is** ☐ **isn't** a good fit for me because ______________________________

On a scale of 1–5, how important is this?
(circle one) 1 2 3 4 5

This college is located in ______________ *(the city, the suburbs, a college town, the country)*

This ☐ **is** ☐ **isn't** a good fit for me because ______________________________

On a scale of 1–5, how important is this?
(circle one) 1 2 3 4 5

This college is located in the ______________ *region of the country.*

This ☐ **is** ☐ **isn't** a good fit for me because ______________________________

On a scale of 1–5, how important is this?
(circle one) 1 2 3 4 5

The size of this college is ______________

This ☐ **is** ☐ **isn't** a good fit for me because ______________________________

On a scale of 1–5, how important is this?
(circle one) 1 2 3 4 5

The social scene consists mostly of ______________________________

This ☐ **is** ☐ **isn't** a good fit for me because ______________________________

On a scale of 1–5, how important is this?
(circle one) 1 2 3 4 5

Most students like to (culture, leisure) ______________________________

This ☐ **is** ☐ **isn't** a good fit for me because ______________________________

On a scale of 1–5, how important is this?
(circle one) 1 2 3 4 5

Outdoor recreational activities for students at this college include ______________________________

This ☐ **is** ☐ **isn't** a good fit for me because ______________________________

On a scale of 1–5, how important is this?
(circle one) 1 2 3 4 5

Politically, most of the students at this college are ______________________________

This ☐ **is** ☐ **isn't** a good fit for me because ______________________________

On a scale of 1–5, how important is this?
(circle one) 1 2 3 4 5

Most of the students at this college are from ______________________________

This ☐ **is** ☐ **isn't** a good fit for me because ______________________________

On a scale of 1–5, how important is this?
(circle one) 1 2 3 4 5

The weather in this region is ______________________________

This ☐ **is** ☐ **isn't** a good fit for me because ______________________________

On a scale of 1–5, how important is this?
(circle one) 1 2 3 4 5

The distance from my family's home to this college is ______________

This ☐ **is** ☐ **isn't** a good fit for me because ______________________________

On a scale of 1–5, how important is this?
(circle one) 1 2 3 4 5

The tuition at this college is ______________

This ☐ **is** ☐ **isn't** a good fit for me because ______________________________

On a scale of 1–5, how important is this?
(circle one) 1 2 3 4 5

☐ **will** ☐ **won't** need financial aid.

This ☐ **is** ☐ **isn't** a good fit for me because ______________________________

On a scale of 1–5, how important is this?
(circle one) 1 2 3 4 5

My three favorite things about this college are

1. ______________
2. ______________
3. ______________

My three least favorite things about this college are

1. ______________
2. ______________
3. ______________

COLLEGE OVERVIEW WORKSHEET

FOR ______________________
COLLEGE

Using college Web sites and print and online resources, compare the college's high and low stats and percentages to yours to determine if this school is a high-reach, middle-reach, or safety school for you. (See pages 29–30 for more detailed instructions on how to complete both sides of this worksheet.)

test scores

SAT	Verbal	High______	Low______	My Score______
	Math	High______	Low______	My Score______
	Writing	High______	Low______	My Score______
SAT II	______	High______	Low______	My Score______
SAT II	______	High______	Low______	My Score______
SAT II	______	High______	Low______	My Score______
SAT II	______	High______	Low______	My Score______
ACT	English	High______	Low______	My Score______
ACT	Math	High______	Low______	My Score______
ACT	Reading	High______	Low______	My Score______
ACT	Science	High______	Low______	My Score______
ACT	Writing	High______	Low______	My Score______
AP	Composite	High______	Low______	My Score______
AP	______	High______	Low______	My Score______
AP	______	High______	Low______	My Score______
AP	______	High______	Low______	My Score______
AP	______	High______	Low______	My Score______

grade point average
High______ Low______ My GPA______

class rank
Top______ Percentile______ My Rank______

additional attributes *sought by this college*______

My attributes______

percent of applicants accepted ______%

- ☐ I am in the top 30 percent of applicants
- ☐ I am in the middle 40 percent of applicants
- ☐ I am in the bottom 30 percent of applicants

- ☐ This college is a high-reach choice.
- ☐ This college is a middle-reach choice.
- ☐ This college is a safety choice.
- ☐ I am not going to apply to this college.

- ☐ The tuition ($______ per year) is a consideration.
- ☐ The location (______) is a consideration.
- ☐ Other: ______ is a consideration.

NOTES

______

FOR ____________________ COLLEGE

The academic environment at this college is ____________________

This ☐ **is** ☐ **isn't** a good fit for me because ____________________

On a scale of 1–5, how important is this?
(circle one) 1 2 3 4 5

The extracurricular activities at this college include ____________________

This ☐ **is** ☐ **isn't** a good fit for me because ____________________

On a scale of 1–5, how important is this?
(circle one) 1 2 3 4 5

This college is located in ____________________ *(the city, the suburbs, a college town, the country)*

This ☐ **is** ☐ **isn't** a good fit for me because ____________________

On a scale of 1–5, how important is this?
(circle one) 1 2 3 4 5

This college is located in the ____________________ *region of the country.*

This ☐ **is** ☐ **isn't** a good fit for me because ____________________

On a scale of 1–5, how important is this?
(circle one) 1 2 3 4 5

The size of this college is ____________________

This ☐ **is** ☐ **isn't** a good fit for me because ____________________

On a scale of 1–5, how important is this?
(circle one) 1 2 3 4 5

The social scene consists mostly of ____________________

This ☐ **is** ☐ **isn't** a good fit for me because ____________________

On a scale of 1–5, how important is this?
(circle one) 1 2 3 4 5

Most students like to (culture, leisure) ____________________

This ☐ **is** ☐ **isn't** a good fit for me because ____________________

On a scale of 1–5, how important is this?
(circle one) 1 2 3 4 5

Outdoor recreational activities for students at this college include ____________________

This ☐ **is** ☐ **isn't** a good fit for me because ____________________

On a scale of 1–5, how important is this?
(circle one) 1 2 3 4 5

Politically, most of the students at this college are ____________________

This ☐ **is** ☐ **isn't** a good fit for me because ____________________

On a scale of 1–5, how important is this?
(circle one) 1 2 3 4 5

Most of the students at this college are from ____________________

This ☐ **is** ☐ **isn't** a good fit for me because ____________________

On a scale of 1–5, how important is this?
(circle one) 1 2 3 4 5

The weather in this region is ____________________

This ☐ **is** ☐ **isn't** a good fit for me because ____________________

On a scale of 1–5, how important is this?
(circle one) 1 2 3 4 5

The distance from my family's home to this college is ____________________

This ☐ **is** ☐ **isn't** a good fit for me because ____________________

On a scale of 1–5, how important is this?
(circle one) 1 2 3 4 5

The tuition at this college is ____________________

This ☐ **is** ☐ **isn't** a good fit for me because ____________________

On a scale of 1–5, how important is this?
(circle one) 1 2 3 4 5

☐ **will** ☐ **won't** need financial aid.

This ☐ **is** ☐ **isn't** a good fit for me because ____________________

On a scale of 1–5, how important is this?
(circle one) 1 2 3 4 5

My three favorite things about this college are

1. ____________________
2. ____________________
3. ____________________

My three least favorite things about this college are

1. ____________________
2. ____________________
3. ____________________

SCHOOLS I PLAN TO VISIT AND/OR RESEARCH FURTHER WORKSHEET

The colleges you put on this list are still in the running for your final list. This is the worksheet on which you note new information and answer any remaining questions to help you eliminate or keep a particular college on your list. (See page 30 for more detailed instructions on how to complete this worksheet.)

Name ______________________

Web site ______________________

☐ **High-reach** ☐ **Middle-reach** ☐ **Safety**

NOTES ______________________

Name ______________________

Web site ______________________

☐ **High-reach** ☐ **Middle-reach** ☐ **Safety**

NOTES ______________________

Name ______________________

Web site ______________________

☐ **High-reach** ☐ **Middle-reach** ☐ **Safety**

NOTES ______________________

Name ______________________

Web site ______________________

☐ **High-reach** ☐ **Middle-reach** ☐ **Safety**

NOTES ______________________

Name ______________________

Web site ______________________

☐ **High-reach** ☐ **Middle-reach** ☐ **Safety**

NOTES ______________________

Name ______________________

Web site ______________________

☐ **High-reach** ☐ **Middle-reach** ☐ **Safety**

NOTES ______________________

Name ______________________

Web site ______________________

☐ **High-reach** ☐ **Middle-reach** ☐ **Safety**

NOTES ______________________

Name ______________________

Web site ______________________

☐ **High-reach** ☐ **Middle-reach** ☐ **Safety**

NOTES ______________________

Name ______________________

Web site ______________________

☐ **High-reach** ☐ **Middle-reach** ☐ **Safety**

NOTES ______________________

Name ______________________

Web site ______________________

☐ **High-reach** ☐ **Middle-reach** ☐ **Safety**

NOTES ______________________

COLLEGE APPLICANT WORKSHEET — REDUX

If everything else were equal, I would be happiest spending four-plus years at a school . . . (check the appropriate boxes)
(See page 30 for more detailed instructions on how to complete this worksheet.)

environment

- ☐ in a big city
- ☐ in a college town
- ☐ in the suburbs adjacent to a big city
- ☐ in the country
- ☐ no preference

Why? ______________________________

Pros and cons? ______________________________

On a scale of 1–5, how important is this?
(circle one) 1 2 3 4 5

weather

- ☐ where it's sunny all the time
- ☐ where you see a change of seasons
- ☐ where the four seasons are rain, hail, sleet, and snow
- ☐ no preference

Why? ______________________________

Pros and cons? ______________________________

On a scale of 1–5, how important is this?
(circle one) 1 2 3 4 5

size

- ☐ with fewer than 2,000 undergrads
- ☐ with between 2,000 and 5,000 undergrads
- ☐ with between 5,000 and 10,000 undergrads
- ☐ with between 10,000 and 20,000 undergrads
- ☐ with more than 20,000 undergrads
- ☐ no preference

Why? ______________________________

Pros and cons? ______________________________

On a scale of 1–5, how important is this?
(circle one) 1 2 3 4 5

region

- ☐ in the Northeast/Mid-Atlantic states
- ☐ in the Southeast/Gulf states
- ☐ in the Midwest
- ☐ in the Northwest
- ☐ in the Southwest
- ☐ in the West/Pacific Northwest
- ☐ in ______________________________ (city or state)
- ☐ no preference

Why? ______________________________

Pros and cons? ______________________________

On a scale of 1–5, how important is this?
(circle one) 1 2 3 4 5

accessibility

- ☐ less than two hours from my family's house
- ☐ two to six hours away
- ☐ less than a day's drive away
- ☐ at least a plane ride away
- ☐ no preference

Why? ______________________________

Pros and cons? ______________________________

On a scale of 1–5, how important is this?
(circle one) 1 2 3 4 5

living arrangements

- ☐ where everyone lives in dorms
- ☐ where living in Greek (fraternity/sorority) housing is an option
- ☐ where alternative/theme housing is an option
- ☐ where living off campus is an option
- ☐ where people live with their families and commute
- ☐ no preference

Why? ______________________________

Pros and cons? ______________________________

On a scale of 1–5, how important is this?
(circle one) 1 2 3 4 5

Continued on next page

COLLEGE APPLICANT WORKSHEET — REDUX

social

- ☐ where most of the social scene is on campus
- ☐ where most of the social scene is off campus
- ☐ where weekends revolve around football games
- ☐ where the social scene revolves around the Greek system
- ☐ where there are many extracurricular organizations
- ☐ where weekends are made for road trips
- ☐ where alternative is the norm
- ☐ where the Grateful Dead is still very much alive
- ☐ no preference

Why? ______________________________

____

____

Pros and cons? ______________________________

____

____

On a scale of 1–5, how important is this?
(circle one) 1 2 3 4 5

culture

- ☐ where you can hear live music
- ☐ where you can visit museums
- ☐ where you can see live theater
- ☐ where watching football is considered a cultural outing
- ☐ where you can eat out at nice restaurants
- ☐ where you can shop

Why? ______________________________

____

____

Pros and cons? ______________________________

____

____

On a scale of 1–5, how important is this?
(circle one) 1 2 3 4 5

politics

- ☐ where students are conservative
- ☐ where students are liberal
- ☐ where students do not define themselves by their politics
- ☐ where religion plays a role in daily life
- ☐ no preference

Why? ______________________________

____

____

Pros and cons? ______________________________

____

____

On a scale of 1–5, how important is this?
(circle one) 1 2 3 4 5

academics

- ☐ where studying is everything and students fight for their class rank
- ☐ where students take their classes very seriously but the environment isn't quite so competitive
- ☐ where students are invested in their studies but academics don't rule their lives
- ☐ where showing up for class is not a requirement to pass

Sorry, "no preference" is not an option on this one. You have to make a decision here.

Why? ______________________________

____

____

Pros and cons? ______________________________

____

____

On a scale of 1–5, how important is this?
(circle one) 1 2 3 4 5

COLLEGE APPLICANT WORKSHEET — REDUX

ADDITIONAL THOUGHTS (Use this space to note other criteria you want to consider as you put together your list.)

PARENT WORKSHEET — REDUX

If everything else were equal, I would be happiest seeing my son/daughter spend four-plus years at a school . . . (check the appropriate boxes)
(See page 30 for more detailed instructions on how to complete this worksheet.)

environment

- ☐ in a big city
- ☐ in a college town
- ☐ in the suburbs adjacent to a big city
- ☐ in the country
- ☐ no preference

Why? ______________________

Pros and cons? ______________________

On a scale of 1–5, how important is this?
(circle one) 1 2 3 4 5

weather

- ☐ where it's sunny all the time
- ☐ where you see a change of seasons
- ☐ where the four seasons are rain, hail, sleet, and snow
- ☐ no preference

Why? ______________________

Pros and cons? ______________________

On a scale of 1–5, how important is this?
(circle one) 1 2 3 4 5

size

- ☐ with fewer than 2,000 undergrads
- ☐ with between 2,000 and 5,000 undergrads
- ☐ with between 5,000 and 10,000 undergrads
- ☐ with between 10,000 and 20,000 undergrads
- ☐ with more than 20,000 undergrads
- ☐ no preference

Why? ______________________

Pros and cons? ______________________

On a scale of 1–5, how important is this?
(circle one) 1 2 3 4 5

region

- ☐ in the Northeast/Mid-Atlantic states
- ☐ in the Southeast/Gulf states
- ☐ in the Midwest
- ☐ in the Northwest
- ☐ in the Southwest
- ☐ in the West/Pacific Northwest
- ☐ in ______________________ (city or state)
- ☐ no preference

Why? ______________________

Pros and cons? ______________________

On a scale of 1–5, how important is this?
(circle one) 1 2 3 4 5

accessibility

- ☐ less than two hours from my family's house
- ☐ two to six hours away
- ☐ less than a day's drive away
- ☐ at least a plane ride away
- ☐ no preference

Why? ______________________

Pros and cons? ______________________

On a scale of 1–5, how important is this?
(circle one) 1 2 3 4 5

living arrangements

- ☐ where everyone lives in dorms
- ☐ where living in Greek (fraternity/sorority) housing is an option
- ☐ where alternative/theme housing is an option
- ☐ where living off campus is an option
- ☐ where people live with their families and commute
- ☐ no preference

Why? ______________________

Pros and cons? ______________________

On a scale of 1–5, how important is this?
(circle one) 1 2 3 4 5

Continued on next page

PARENT WORKSHEET — REDUX

social

- ☐ where most of the social scene is on campus
- ☐ where most of the social scene is off campus
- ☐ where weekends revolve around football games
- ☐ where the social scene revolves around the Greek system
- ☐ where there are many extracurricular organizations
- ☐ where weekends are made for road trips
- ☐ where alternative is the norm
- ☐ where the Grateful Dead is still very much alive
- ☐ no preference

Why? ______________________________

____

____

Pros and cons? ______________________________

____

____

On a scale of 1–5, how important is this?
(circle one) 1 2 3 4 5

culture

- ☐ where you can hear live music
- ☐ where you can visit museums
- ☐ where you can see live theater
- ☐ where watching football is considered a cultural outing
- ☐ where you can eat out at nice restaurants
- ☐ where you can shop

Why? ______________________________

____

____

Pros and cons? ______________________________

____

____

On a scale of 1–5, how important is this?
(circle one) 1 2 3 4 5

politics

- ☐ where students are conservative
- ☐ where students are liberal
- ☐ where students do not define themselves by their politics
- ☐ where religion plays a role in daily life
- ☐ no preference

Why? ______________________________

____

____

Pros and cons? ______________________________

____

____

On a scale of 1–5, how important is this?
(circle one) 1 2 3 4 5

academics

- ☐ where studying is everything and students fight for their class rank
- ☐ where students take their classes very seriously but the environment isn't quite so competitive
- ☐ where students are invested in their studies but academics don't rule their lives
- ☐ where showing up for class is not a requirement to pass

Sorry, "no preference" is not an option on this one. You have to make a decision here.

Why? ______________________________

____

____

Pros and cons? ______________________________

____

____

On a scale of 1–5, how important is this?
(circle one) 1 2 3 4 5

PARENT WORKSHEET — REDUX

ADDITIONAL THOUGHTS (Use this space to note other criteria you want to consider as you put together your list.)

THE FINAL LIST — WHERE I'M APPLYING TO COLLEGE WORKSHEET

This is it! You should apply to a minimum of five but no more than eight colleges. (See page 30 for more detailed instructions on how to complete this worksheet.)

safety

Name ______________________________
Web site ______________________________
If applicable: ☐ **1st choice** ☐ **2nd choice** ☐ **3rd choice** (overall)

Name ______________________________
Web site ______________________________
If applicable: ☐ **1st choice** ☐ **2nd choice** ☐ **3rd choice** (overall)

Name ______________________________
Web site ______________________________
If applicable: ☐ **1st choice** ☐ **2nd choice** ☐ **3rd choice** (overall)

Notes ______________________________

____

____

____

____

middle-reach

Name ______________________________
Web site ______________________________
If applicable: ☐ **1st choice** ☐ **2nd choice** ☐ **3rd choice** (overall)

Name ______________________________
Web site ______________________________
If applicable: ☐ **1st choice** ☐ **2nd choice** ☐ **3rd choice** (overall)

Name ______________________________
Web site ______________________________
If applicable: ☐ **1st choice** ☐ **2nd choice** ☐ **3rd choice** (overall)

Notes ______________________________

____

____

____

____

high-reach

Name ______________________________
Web site ______________________________
If applicable: ☐ **1st choice** ☐ **2nd choice** ☐ **3rd choice** (overall)

Name ______________________________
Web site ______________________________
If applicable: ☐ **1st choice** ☐ **2nd choice** ☐ **3rd choice** (overall)

Name ______________________________
Web site ______________________________
If applicable: ☐ **1st choice** ☐ **2nd choice** ☐ **3rd choice** (overall)

Notes ______________________________

____

____

____

____

- Remember, you need to have at least three schools from the combined middle-reach and safety categories. (If you have two safety schools, you need only one middle-reach school and vice versa.
- Don't forget to update the checklists on the college folders at the back of this book!

CHAPTER 2: GETTING IN — MAKING YOURSELF THE IDEAL CANDIDATE

Everyone wants to know the secret formula colleges use to determine which applicants they will accept and which ones they will deny. While it is nearly impossible to pinpoint the exact weight colleges give to each component of your application, the order in which they rank the components is very clear. In order of importance: grades, standardized test scores, extracurricular activities, community service, and summer activities are all seriously considered and reviewed by college admissions. (This order does not apply to someone who is being recruited for an athletic or other type of scholarship.)

In this chapter you will find information on how to make the most of your curriculum, improve your test scores, and get involved in activities that will make you a good college admissions candidate.

IN THIS CHAPTER

- Grades
    - A's versus AP's
- Standardized tests
    - The SAT versus the ACT
    - The SAT I (also known as the New SAT)
    - The ACT
    - SAT II subject tests
    - AP exams
    - Test-prep resources
- Extracurriculars
    - Quality versus quantity
    - What if you have no idea what interests you?
- Community service
    - Long-term commitment versus spring break extravaganza
    - Community service and your college essay
- Summer activities
    - If money is not an issue
    - Make your summer job work for you
- 4-year worksheets
- The student resumē, AKA the brag sheet
    - Resumē components
    - Creating your resumē
    - Resumē writing and formatting tips
    - Resumē writing resources

GRADES

Given that this is a book on college admissions, you had to know that sooner or later the subject of grades would come up. So just how important are your grades? To put it succinctly, your grades are the single-most important factor in your application (unless you are being recruited for a talent-based scholarship).

There are two critical pieces of information that colleges use to determine the weight of your GPA: your curriculum and your class rank. Your curriculum consists of the classes that you take. Each year, your curriculum should contain all of the core classes: English, math, history, science, and language. As far as colleges are concerned, the more challenging your curriculum, the better. They will be much more impressed with an A in calculus than an A in basket weaving.

You need to work with your college counselor to take the most challenging courses that you can handle — without setting yourself up for failure.

Your class rank indicates where you stand in your class compared to your classmates. This ranking system helps colleges to determine how tough your school's grading system is. If you have a 3.8, but are in the bottom 50 percent of your class, your GPA is going to be viewed differently from someone who has a 3.5 but is in the top 25 percent of the class.

A's versus AP's

What's better — an A or an AP? In a perfect world, you get an A in the AP. In the real world, if you can get a B, take the AP. If you're more likely to get a C, take the regular class and save college-level classes for college.

Not everyone is cut out to take all honors courses or is capable of getting straight A's. Naturally, you want to get the best grades you can. Why settle for a B+, when you can get an A? But if you do your best and you get a B+, then it's okay to be satisfied and remember that you've given it your best effort. That's all anyone can ask of you. Do not make yourself crazy. There are still plenty of good colleges that will be thrilled to have you.

One eighth-grade teacher at a private school informed his students on the first day of school that their grades that year would determine the quality of the rest of their life! His reasoning was that their grades would determine the prep school they would get into, which would determine the college they would get into, which would determine how good of a job they would ultimately get.

This is completely absurd on so many levels. First of all, at this point, the number of applicants admitted to Ivy League colleges is greater from public schools than from private schools. (Gone are the days when attending a New England prep school guaranteed you admission into an Ivy League college.) Secondly, there is no proven correlation between the college a person attends and his or her income after graduation.

STANDARDIZED TESTS

Whatever your opinion of the standardized testing system, it does have its usefulness. It is the only tool that college admissions officers have to judge all of their applicants by the same standard. This is especially beneficial to those students who attend schools with especially stringent grading curves, as well as home-schooled students. The latter benefit because it is impossible for admissions officers not to question the objectivity of a teacher's recommendations and grades when the teacher is also the student's parent.

Colleges are reluctant to give hard and fast rules for the weight they give to standardized test scores. But before you throw yourself into a complete panic over the prospect of taking a standardized test, remember it is only one of several factors that colleges will take into consideration when reviewing your application. In other words, your score is not going to single-handedly destroy the rest of your life, despite the fact that it may feel that way right now.

TIP: Students who get good grades but don't do well on standardized tests sometimes score higher on the ACT than they do on the SAT. This is because the ACT tests students on learned knowledge as opposed to abstract reasoning as the SAT does.

The SAT versus the ACT

There are two types of standardized tests — the SAT and the ACT — that colleges use to evaluate applicants, and almost all colleges will accept either one. The SAT tends to be more popular with the most competitive schools on both coasts, while the ACT is more popular with schools in the Midwest and the South.

However, many schools state that they do not prefer one over the other. Because applying to college is stressful, and this seems like yet another in a long line of life-altering decisions, applicants tend to second-guess colleges on which test to take, convinced that the colleges really do have a preference. If you're concerned, you can always ask the admissions officer at the colleges on your list if they prefer one test over the other. If you're still not satisfied, you can take both tests. However, this seems a bit excessive.

the major differences between the SAT and the ACT

- The writing section is required on the SAT. It is optional on the ACT.
- The ACT is more grammar-intensive than the SAT.
- The ACT includes trigonometry. The SAT covers only arithmetic, algebra I and II, and geometry.
- The ACT has a science section. The SAT does not.
- The SAT counts wrong answers against you. The ACT does not.
- Each SAT section is scored from 200 – 800. Each ACT section is scored from 1 – 36.
- Your final SAT score is the sum of your scores on each section. Your final ACT score is the average of your scores on each section.
- Colleges see all of your SAT scores. Colleges see only your highest ACT score.

The SAT I (also known as the New SAT)

The total time is 200 minutes (not including instruction and breaks), broken down as follows:

- Critical Reading Section — total time: 70 minutes (made up of two 25-minute sections and one 20-minute section)
- Math Section — total time: 70 minutes (made up of two 25-minute sections and one 20-minute section)
- Writing — total time: 60 minutes (made up of one 35-minute section and one 25-minute section)

> I wish I'd known much earlier in my high school career about all the test prep materials available. Seeing the SAT questions for the first time on the morning of the test was a harsh reality.
>
> *– Nate, St. Louis, Mo.*

The ACT

The total time is 205 minutes (not including instruction and breaks), broken down as follows:

- English — made up of one 45-minute section
- Math — made up of one 60-minute section
- Reading — made up of one 35-minute section
- Science — made up of one 35-minute section
- Writing (optional) — made up of one 30-minute section

SAT II subject tests

Much less scary than the New SAT are the SAT Subject Tests, which measure your performance in specific subjects, such as English, math, history, foreign languages, and sciences. You should take the subject tests in June, immediately after you finish the corresponding courses.

Not all colleges require that you take the SAT Subject Tests, although the more competitive schools usually require that you take a minimum of three.

The SAT II Subject Tests are only one hour in length. Like the SAT I, they are scored from 200 – 800.

AP exams

AP exams, which are administered by a department of the College Board called AP Services, offer students the opportunity to receive college credit for courses taken in high school. (Most colleges accept a score of 3 or higher for college credit.) No colleges require you to submit AP exams as part of the admissions process. However, the most competitive schools expect to see at least a couple of AP courses on your transcript and AP exams in your file.

You have the option of withholding your AP exam grade from certain colleges, as well as cancelling your AP exam grade altogether. AP Services must receive a signed letter from you by June 15, requesting that the grade be cancelled or withheld from a specific school or schools. (Since you will not have your AP exam grade by this date, you are left to guess how you think you did.) However, colleges will see on your transcript that you took an AP course, but that no score is available. For more information, visit the College Board Web site at www.collegeboard.com, and type "AP Exams" in the search box.

Depending on the subject, AP exams range in length from two to three hours. AP exams are scored from 1 to 5.

Test-prep resources

There are as many theories out there on the value of prepping for the standardized tests as there are courses being offered. Some test-prep companies promise a 200-point increase, while a very small but vocal contingent argues that there is no real way to improve your score by studying. Fortunately, the vast numbers of students who have significantly improved their scores by prepping for these tests have disproved the latter theory.

For those of you who want to increase your score, there are a plethora of resources at your disposal:

- Classroom and tutorial courses
- Online interactive courses that allow you to take the course and work with a tutor online
- Do-it-yourself prep courses both on the Internet and in books
- Novels written specifically for the purpose of increasing your vocabulary. (Granted, these books may not be the most fascinating reading, but it beats trying to memorize the dictionary.)
- Music designed specifically to help you learn vocabulary (Parents: imagine actually encouraging your child to listen to music.)

It is a good idea to take the PSAT or an SAT practice test before you take the actual SAT. The reason for this is that all of your SAT scores are reported to the colleges on your list. While most colleges take only the best scores, some take an average of all your test scores. By taking a practice test or the PSAT, you can get a pretty clear idea of how well you will perform on the SAT and how much studying you need to do to prepare without the risk of a low score being reported to all the colleges on your list.

TIP: Something to think about: the mere act of taking the test and familiarizing yourself with the format is likely to increase your score a little bit.

taking practice tests

When you take a practice test, simulate the actual test experience as closely as possible by doing the following:

- Set aside a chunk of time during which you will not be disturbed, so that you can complete the test in one sitting, taking no more than a three-minute break every three sections.
- Sit at a desk or a table in a quiet room (not lounging on the sofa in the family room with the TV on).
- Set a timer for the allotted time when you start each section, and stop working when the timer goes off.
- Fill in the worksheet using a pencil as you would on the actual test.
- Snack only during your breaks as you would have to during the actual test.

Once you're finished, don't forget to score yourself. If you got a perfect score: Bravo! You are free to go hang out and contemplate your SAT godliness. For those of you who did not get a perfect score — and don't feel bad, that's just about all of you — your work is not finished. Review and rework the problems you got wrong so you can figure out the correct answer next time. Then review the problems that you got right so you can be certain of how you came up with the correct answer. By doing this, the next time you take the test you will be able to answer those questions more quickly, allowing yourself extra time for the more taxing problems.

online versus paper and pencil tests

For obvious reasons, many of the online prep courses require you to take the quizzes online. In terms of practicing answering questions, there is no problem with this. However, you also need to be comfortable taking the test in the same format as that administered by the College Board. At some point in your practice, you should use a pencil and worksheet so that you become comfortable taking the test this way.

online test-prep resources

Following is a list of the larger test-prep companies — and a couple of the smaller but hot new up-and-comers.

Barron's Test Prep
www.barronstestprep.com
Offering online courses and books for the PSAT, the SAT, and the ACT; Barron has taken the information in its test prep books and uploaded it to the Web. For those who want simply to take practice tests online, this site offers you a place to do it at the ridiculously reasonable price of $11 for six months. When you get your score, you also receive an explanation for each

question, whether your answer was right or wrong. The types of tips and explanations mirror the sample questions on the tests. However, the one drawback is that the questions tend to be a little less complex than those you will find on the SAT.
FINAL WORD: If you're looking for practice, the price is right.

Boston Test Prep

http://sat.bostontestprep.com
Boston Test Prep is purely online, and the company is proud of it — using all the latest information and a streamlined approach to help you prep for the SAT at the affordable price of $99 for three months. Once students take the diagnostic test, they are assigned lessons and quizzes designed to help them improve in their weaker areas. In order to be eligible for the 200-point score increase guarantee, students must be enrolled in the program for at least three months and earn 60,000 prep points. (Each correct quiz answer is worth 100 points; each negative answer costs 25 points. So to be eligible a student needs a minimum of 600 correct answers, provided he or she answers all the questions correctly.) Students can also get tips by reading BTP's blog and find moral support through online interaction with other students. Multitaskers will appreciate the printable vocabulary flashcards they can carry with them.
FINAL WORD: A good test prep service, at a good price.

Kaplan

www.kaptest.com
This test-prep giant offers courses for the GMAT, the ISEE, the MCAT, and of course, the SAT ($399 for a six-month course), the ACT ($299 for a six-month course), AP exams, and the PSAT. Kaplan's online program is definitely one of the best, with features such as customized study plans based on your SAT date, step-by-step explanations of problems, and easy-to-navigate pages. If you need more personal interaction, you can take a classroom course or private tutorial for either the SAT I and/or II, the ACT, or the AP exam. (Kaplan does not offer online courses for the SAT Subject Tests.)
FINAL WORD: It's a little pricey, but if you can afford it, it's money well spent.

Number2.com (free!)

www.number2.com
If you believe the best things in life are free, then check out Number2.com. Offering services for the SAT, the ACT, and the GRE, this company is definitely worth checking out before you haul out your checkbook for one of the more expensive courses. All you need is an e-mail address and you are good to go. Number 2's strength is the math section, although the entire prep course is full of tips and hints. Another unique feature is Number 2's weekly pep talk e-mails. And parents can sign up as "coaches" — and receive updates on their child's progress.
FINAL WORD: If you're on a budget, you can't beat it.

The Official SAT Online Course

http://store.collegeboard.com
On the plus side, the fact that the College Board is the maker of the SAT lends credibility to this prep course ($69 for four months) and its practice tests. On the minus side, this same fact would have to make the College Board less inclined to dole out handy test-taking tricks of the variety that another test-prep company might offer. What you do get is six practice tests (that's more than 600 questions, written by the College Board) and personalized feedback regarding your weak areas. However, the essay section of this course may not be a good gauge of how you'll do on the actual test, since it is scored by a computer, not people, as it is on the actual test.
FINAL WORD: If you're looking for straight-up practice, this is the place to go.

PrepMe

www.prepme.com
Founded in 2005 by graduates of the University of Chicago, Cal Tech, and Stanford, PrepMe is a newcomer on the test-prep scene, offering courses for the SAT, the ACT, and the PSAT. Unlike Kaplan and Princeton Review, which also offer classroom courses, PrepMe is online only, with one-on-one programs ($499 for four months) tailored to each individual. The program gauges your strengths and weakness so that you get the help you need and don't have to waste time on things you've already mastered. Another major plus is that, despite the online orientation of the course, the practice tests are taken with pencil and paper to simulate the real SAT experience. PrepMe's new "Precocious" prep program is designed to get sixth-, seventh-, and eighth-graders into the game early. *The Official SAT Study Guide* is included in the price of the course.
FINAL WORD: It's a little pricier than some of the others, but it's a great course.

Continued on next page

online test-prep resources (continued)

The Princeton Review

www.review.com

Another test prep-giant, the Princeton Review offers courses for just about every standardized test there is, including the SAT I and II, the ACT, the PSAT, and AP exams. In addition to its very popular classroom programs, Princeton Review offers three versions of its online courses for both the SAT and the ACT, with prices ranging from $79 – $599. Each course is interactive, with the most expensive course touting live online class sessions with a tutor. The site itself is well designed and user friendly — Princeton Review even offers podcasts for you to listen to while on the go. Princeton Review does not offer online courses for the SAT II. However, it does offer classroom courses, private tutoring, and test-prep books for individual SAT Subject Tests.

FINAL WORD: For test-taking strategies, this is the place to go.

test-prep books

Barron's SAT 2400: Aiming for the Perfect Score

Barron's Educational Series ($16.99)

According to the College Entrance Exam Advisors and Educators, this is the only book to "get the Writing Skills strategies correct" and it also beats out the competition in both the reading comprehension and essay categories. Where this book falls short is its lack of practice tests.

FINAL WORD: The perfect book for perfectionists — but buy a practice book to go with it.

Kaplan SAT 2400

Kaplan ($20.00)

Designed to help high scorers score even higher, this book has a math section that is particularly useful since it provides tips for even the most challenging problems. Another standout feature of this book is the essay section, which provides students with specific tips by walking them through the process of improving a mediocre essay. The one drawback to this book is the lack of practice tests.

FINAL WORD: A great choice for those going for a 2400 — but buy a practice book to go with it.

McGraw-Hill's SAT 1

McGraw-Hill ($15.95)

This monster of a book is best for those who have a lot of time to prep for the SAT and who want tons and tons of practice. All practice test questions provide an explanation, so you can learn why you got an answer right or wrong. This book does a great job of covering (sometimes ad nauseam) all of the material you will encounter on the test. However, if you're looking for quick tricks and strategies for outsmarting the SAT, you're not going to find them here.

FINAL WORD: If you like to dot every i and cross every t, then this is the book for you.

Princeton Review: Cracking the New SAT

Princeton Review ($19.95)

The next best thing to taking the course, Princeton Review's *Cracking the New SAT* provides numerous tricks and tips to help you outsmart the SAT. While the Joe Bloggs approach of second-guessing the test makers to narrow down your answers is not foolproof, it pays off enough to make it worthwhile for all but the highest scorers. If you buy the version with the CD-Rom, you get seven practice tests instead of three when you buy just the book.

FINAL WORD: If you buy one test-prep book, make it this one.

Up Your Score: The Underground Guide to the SAT

Workman Publishing Company ($11.95)

Definitely the most amusing of the SAT test-prep manuals, *Up Your Score* has been heralded by *The New York Times* as "a guerilla manual to fighting the enemy." The only thing missing from this book is practice tests. However, tips on how to outsmart the SAT abound, along with valuable information on each of the sections.

FINAL WORD: For quick and painless SAT tips, this is as good as it gets — but buy a practice book to go with it.

SAT II subject test-prep books

Kaplan, Princeton Review, Barron's, and of course, the College Board, offer test-prep books for the SAT Subject Tests. If you know you're going to be taking a number of these tests, *The Official Study Guide for All SAT Subject Tests*, which provides practice tests for all 20 subjects, is a good buy. No matter how well you are doing in your class, take a practice test to see how you will do on the SAT Subject Test. Not all schools cover all the material you will encounter on the test, so pick up the corresponding SAT Subject Test study guide so you won't have any surprises when you take the test.

EXTRACURRICULARS

Colleges want students who are going to get involved in the campus community. They used to be a lot more forgiving of a lack of extracurriculars when a student was first in the class, with honors in everything, and scored a perfect SAT. Now they look for candidates who will also give something back to the community on campus and not just soak up resources like a sponge.

Quality versus quantity

Contrary to popular belief, colleges are not impressed by a laundry list of extracurricular activities. Don't sign up for a bunch of clubs just because you think it will look good on your applications — because generally, it won't. Colleges want to see that you can commit to a couple of causes, excel, and show leadership. A couple of activities like this on your resumē will carry a lot more weight than a list of ten activities for which you merely showed up.

You have the best shot of excelling and taking a leadership position by doing something that you genuinely like, so put some thought into what you get involved in. It doesn't really matter whether it's sports, music, band, the school play, the yearbook, the newspaper, student government, the debate team, or community service off campus. Just jump in and get involved.

What if you have no idea what interests you?

If you truly have no clue what interests you, then sign up for a variety of activities freshman and/or sophomore year. You can decide by your junior year which ones you want to fully commit to and which ones you will keep or drop as your time permits. If you've tried every activity on campus and you haven't found one you like, it's time for you to form your own group around whatever activity you are most passionate about. Or consider making community service your extracurricular activity. The most important thing is that you do something — colleges look for students who make the most of their time by doing something worthwhile. No sitting on the sidelines!

TIP: If you're interested in finding community service opportunities, check out National Student Partnerships (www.nspnet.org), which provides students with excellent volunteering opportunities in numerous cities across the country.

COMMUNITY SERVICE

Many high schools now require you to perform a certain number of hours of community service. Since you are required to do it anyway, why not find a cause you really believe in rather than having to spend a Saturday picking up trash along with the rest of your class (not that there's anything wrong with that)?

Long-term commitment versus spring-break extravaganza

When it comes time to fill out their applications, students love to pepper their applications with community service. Colleges have caught on and now ask how many hours per week, month, or year you actually spend (or spent) on your activities, as well as what type of initiative you took and if you held a leadership role.

Once you find a cause you believe in, make a commitment to stick with it for a year, or at the very least six months, during which time you should look for every opportunity to take initiative and show leadership. This type of commitment carries a lot more weight with colleges than the day you spend with your class taking underprivileged children to the zoo. (It's not that this isn't a worthwhile and rewarding thing to do. But it doesn't show much initiative, leadership, or commitment on your part.)

Community service and your college essay

Many applicants write their admissions essays on the week/weekend they spent helping build a house in an impoverished country. There's no question that this is a noble and possibly life-changing endeavor. But put yourself in the shoes of the admissions officer for a moment. He or she has to read essay upon essay upon essay, and every third one is on the same life-changing experience. The subject can't help but grow tiresome.

By all means, do community service and put it on your activities sheet. But unless your community service experience shows commitment, initiative, and leadership, seriously consider finding another topic for your essay.

Remember, when it's all said and done, the whole point of doing community service is not to put it on your application. It's an opportunity for you to get outside of yourself and give something back to the community, and, hopefully, to grow in the process.

SUMMER ACTIVITIES

School's out, which means it's time to while away the summer, bask in the sunshine, and work on your tan, right? Wrong! You can give yourself a week or two to decompress, but after that, it's time to get back in the game.

If money is not an issue

- Get an internship in a field you are interested in.
- Find a community service project that you believe in and get involved (see page 67).
- Enroll in a summer camp for your favorite activity (athletics, art, music, drama, etc.).
- Go abroad for the summer through a foreign-exchange program.

Make your summer job work for you

Many students who don't hold down a job during the school year work in the summertime to save money for college or to have extra spending money. Even if your parents are springing for your college tuition, it's a good idea to start putting aside some spending money for college. You won't have your mom cooking dinners for you, and cafeteria food can get old fast, so it's nice to have the cash to go out to dinner once in a while.

Some students worry that they are going to be penalized because they have to work and do not have time to participate in the same number of activities as someone who does not have to work. Holding down a job is a valid reason for not being able to participate in other activities. Colleges will not penalize you for having to work. In many cases, having a job can work in your favor since it shows you are able to take on responsibility. Get a job in a field you are interested in to gain experience. Look for a job that gives you the opportunity to:

- Show commitment
- Take initiative
- Take on responsibility
- Develop leadership skills

4-YEAR WORKSHEETS

Fill out the worksheets on the following pages at the end of each school year. In addition to recording the subjects you studied and your final grade in each course, be sure to list all of your activities, noting the amount of time dedicated to each endeavor. (This information will come in handy when it comes time to create your high school resumē and to fill out your college applications.) Use the notes section to record the details of any noteworthy events or projects (academic or extracurricular) that you may want to refer to when it comes time to write your essays and short-answer question responses.

> Get involved, be involved, stay involved with activities, community, and things that are most important to you, because that — beyond your grades — can make you an ideal candidate for a school.
>
> *–Jessica, Portland, Maine*

Job safety

Be smart about the kind of job you get. No job (or amount of money) is worth jeopardizing your personal safety. According to the National Consumer League, the five most dangerous jobs for teenagers are the following:

1. Agriculture: fieldwork and processing
2. Working construction, especially at heights
3. Landscaping, gardening, and lawn mowing
4. Driving/operating forklifts, tractors, and ATVs
5. Selling door-to-door

For more information on job safety for teenagers, visit the National Consumer League Web site at www.nclnet.org/labor/childlabor/.

9TH-GRADE WORKSHEET

Record your academic and extracurricular accomplishments on this worksheet.

9th-grade GPA ____________

Subject ____________ Grade ______ Subject ____________ Grade ______

Subject ____________ Grade ______ Subject ____________ Grade ______

Subject ____________ Grade ______ Subject ____________ Grade ______

Subject ____________ Grade ______ Subject ____________ Grade ______

awards

leadership positions

extracurricular activities

Art

Clubs

Music

Sports

Theater

Other

community service

jobs

summer activities

travel experiences

interests

notes

10TH-GRADE WORKSHEET

Record your academic and extracurricular accomplishments on this worksheet.

10th-grade GPA ____________________

Subject ________	Grade ________	Subject ________	Grade ________
Subject ________	Grade ________	Subject ________	Grade ________
Subject ________	Grade ________	Subject ________	Grade ________
Subject ________	Grade ________	Subject ________	Grade ________

awards

leadership positions

extracurricular activities

Art

Clubs

Music

Sports

Theater

Other

community service

jobs

summer activities

travel experiences

interests

notes

11TH-GRADE WORKSHEET

Record your academic and extracurricular accomplishments on this worksheet.

11th-grade GPA ____________________

Subject ____________________ Grade __________ Subject ____________________ Grade __________

Subject ____________________ Grade __________ Subject ____________________ Grade __________

Subject ____________________ Grade __________ Subject ____________________ Grade __________

Subject ____________________ Grade __________ Subject ____________________ Grade __________

awards

leadership positions

extracurricular activities

Art

Clubs

Music

Sports

Theater

Other

community service

jobs

summer activities

travel experiences

interests

notes

12TH-GRADE WORKSHEET

Record your academic and extracurricular accomplishments on this worksheet.

12th-grade GPA ______________

Subject ______________ Grade ______ Subject ______________ Grade ______

Subject ______________ Grade ______ Subject ______________ Grade ______

Subject ______________ Grade ______ Subject ______________ Grade ______

Subject ______________ Grade ______ Subject ______________ Grade ______

awards

leadership positions

extracurricular activities

Art

Clubs

Music

Sports

Theater

Other

community service

jobs

summer activities

travel experiences

interests

notes

THE STUDENT RESUMÉ, AKA THE BRAG SHEET

While you will not see this term listed on any of your college applications, the student resumē is an invaluable tool for those writing your recommendations. It makes their job much easier since the resumē allows them to see all of your accomplishments, activities, honors, and awards at a glance. The less time your teachers need to spend getting a sense of you, the more time they can spend actually writing your recommendation, which means they will most likely do a better job.

Resumé components

Your name
Your phone number
Your e-mail address

- Academic awards/honors
- Extracurricular activities
- Special interests
- Community service
- Summer experiences
- Jobs

Creating your resumé

Use your 4-year worksheets (pages 69–72) to put together your high school resumē. You may want to write the document by hand first. However, the final version that you give to teachers and colleges should be typed.

Once you've broken down your achievements into the appropriate sections (see resumē components) and subdivided them by category (for example, drama, hockey, lacrosse), list them with the most important activities/accomplishments first. Then, within each subdivided category, list your activities/accomplishments chronologically.

Do not include headings for which you have no achievements. For example, if you have not won any academic awards or honors, do not include "Academic Awards/Honors" on your resumē. Or if you've received honors but not awards, title that section "Academic Honors."

For extracurricular activities, community service, summer experiences, and jobs, be sure to list the amount of time you committed to the activity and any leadership positions you held. Do not include filler items such as the required day of community service with your class (an exception to this would be if you held a leadership position for the activity or took on additional responsibility).

Generally the resumē contains items from your high school career. However, if you have a noteworthy achievement from earlier in your academic career, by all means include it. But again, do not include mediocre items simply to fill space.

Resumé writing and formatting tips

- Check out *101 Best Resumēs* or a similar title to study the proper formatting and wording style of resumēs.
- Keep your resumē to one page (two at the absolute most).
- Use a font that is easy to read in a standard size (11 or 12 point). If your resumē is running short (or long), increase (or decrease) your font accordingly, within the 11-to-12 point range. You can also decrease or increase the margins by a fraction of an inch on the sides, top, and bottom.
- Do not go crazy with underlining, using italics, or making words bold. (Bold style is fine for headings and subheadings, but should be avoided in the text of your resumē. If you must use it for text, do so very sparingly.)
- Err on the side of simplicity with the design of your resumē. (An exception would be if you have a special interest in art or another creative area.)
- Do not use the first person "I" in your resumē — use bullet points and start each section with a verb.
- Be specific about your accomplishments and activities.
- Do not be afraid of blank space — your resumē will have a much bigger impact if it contains a few really solid achievements. Using a lot of unimpressive filler items that the reader must sift through will only take away from your accomplishments.
- Have a college counselor, parent, and/or friend proofread your resumē (typos will look just as bad to your teachers as they do to college admissions officers).

Resumé writing resources

Following is a list of resumē-writing resources. If you do use one of these services, be sure not to let the writer make your resumē so slick that you come off looking too perfectly packaged. While colleges want to see a clean and correct document that outlines your accomplishments, they can be put off by something that looks too professional, since that makes it appear that you had help.

Resumē Edge

www.resumeedge.com

A division of Essay Edge, Resumē Edge crafts polished resumēs, tailored to your achievements, for $139.95 each. If you already have a resumē but think it needs to be overhauled, you can take advantage of Resumē Edge's editing services — a writer will completely redo your resumē for $119.95. You also have the option of adding a cover letter to either of these packages for an extra $60. If you need help but are concerned about the cost, check out the Resumē Review Service. For $49.95, you can have your resumē critiqued by a certified professional resumē writer.

FINAL WORD: If you're at a loss, you'll find plenty of help here.

Resumē Writers

www.resumewriters.com

For $149.95, Resumē Writers will deliver a student resumē in 72 hours — with a satisfaction guarantee. All you have to do is fill out the form and a professional resumē writer will take it from there, creating a resumē that enhances your achievements. If you're trying to make a good impression on the teachers writing your recommendations, you may want to take advantage of the Student Resumē and Cover Letter package for $199.95. The company also offers 24-hour rush service (an additional $50), will deliver hard copies (ten for $20), and will send your resumē on a disc (an additional $20), which is a great idea if you want to update your resumē later.

FINAL WORD: This is one of the best in the biz.

Resumē Help (free!)

www.resume-help-org

Need help but don't feel like spending money to get it? Check out this resumē-writing site, which offers general and student-specific resumē writing tips. The site includes a college-admissions resumē sample, as well as tips on design, proofreading, and how to make an impact using action words and bullet points. The FAQ section answers such practical questions as whether or not to staple your resumē and what type and font size to use.

FINAL WORD: A great place to get started writing your resumē.

101 Best Resumēs

McGraw-Hill ($12.95)

While this book is targeted primarily to those seeking jobs rather than admission to college, *101 Best Resumēs* is a great source for ideas on how to format and design your resumē. If you are a person who learns best by example, then you will find plenty of information here to jumpstart your own resumē. All of the resumēs in this book are written by certified professional resumē writers.

FINAL WORD: Until someone comes out with *101 Best Student Resumēs*, this book is your best bet for examples on what a resumē should look like and how it should read.

The Elements of Resumē Style

American Management Association ($9.95)

Another book that is primarily targeted to those in the job market, *The Elements of Style* contains plenty of valuable information for students on composing a properly formatted resumē that gets results. It covers everything from how to format your resumē — and why you undermine your accomplishments by accentuating everything — to what type of language will have the most impact.

FINAL WORD: If you can see beyond the job-world advice, this book will walk you through the entire process of creating your resumē.

CHAPTER 3: TIMELINES, DEADLINES, AND TO-DO LISTS

This chapter is all about getting organized, staying on task, and making sure you don't forget any of those all-important deadlines. Freshmen through seniors will find helpful scheduling tips to get their school years off to a good start. A section on test deadlines alerts students in each grade to standardized test registration deadlines. Prepared to-do lists for every grade and every semester and fill-in-the-blank monthly to-do lists will ensure that nothing gets overlooked during these college-prep years.

IN THIS CHAPTER

9th GRADE — SCHEDULING TIPS

You have to study for a test in biology, finish a history report, and write a paper for English. Plus you have more algebraic equations to do than you can even count, and you're supposed to learn how to conjugate all of the irregular verbs for a Spanish quiz — all by tomorrow. Welcome to high school, where there's more work, more activities, more distractions, and often a lot more fun. To get it all done, you need to learn how to manage your time very carefully.

How do you do this?

plan ahead

- At the start of the school year, make a list of all of your classes, activities, and jobs, and then number them in order of priority with one as the most important. Anything you get a grade in should be at the top of your list, with core classes (English, history, math, science) given the highest priority. If you have a conflict, you'll have an easier time deciding what to do if you know which item is more important.

create a routine

- Create a weekly calendar so you can see at a glance what you need to get done and where your time is going.
- Make a daily to-do list of homework assignments and tasks, then number them in order of importance. Make sure the most important items on your list get the most (or best) attention.
- Do your homework at the same time and in the same spot each day — sitting at a table or a desk, rather than lounging on the sofa.
- Stay focused on the task at hand. Things **not** to do while you are studying:
    - Watch TV.
    - Listen to music.
    - Send/receive text messages.
    - Talk on the phone.

know what to do when

- Determine when you are the most alert and reserve that time for studying.
- Use your study halls wisely — it's a novel idea but use your study halls to study rather than to goof off with friends.
- Try to set aside 20 minutes each day to read purely for your own enjoyment. (This should always fall below homework and studying on the to-do list.)

Test deadlines

Consider taking the SAT II Subject Tests in math and/or biology. The registration deadline is in late March/April for the May test. The registration deadline is in late April/May for the June test.

the SAT subject test

Why so soon you ask? The best time to take the SAT Subject Test is immediately following the completion of the course in that subject, when all of the information is still fresh in your brain. If you're taking a course now, putting off that subject test until you are older, and theoretically wiser, is not likely to pay off.

The more competitive colleges require that you take three subject tests. If you don't take the subject test(s) now, know that you are going to have to take other, possibly harder, subject tests later.

The catch: All of your SAT test scores are submitted to the colleges on your list — so if biology (for example) just isn't your subject and you are pretty sure you are going to bomb the test, then don't take it.

9th GRADE — FALL TO-DO LIST

☐ Study hard to get the best grades I can!
Gone are the days when you could slack until your junior year and then impress colleges (and blow away teachers, counselors, and parents) when your GPA suddenly skyrocketed to a 4.0. Colleges can't help but wonder what you were (or most likely, were not) doing during your freshman and sophomore years.

☐ Get involved on campus! Try something completely new!

- ☐ Try out for sports teams.
- ☐ Join the yearbook or newspaper staff.
- ☐ Audition for the school musical.
- ☐ Run for student government.
- ☐ other ______________________

☐ Find a cause and volunteer.

☐ Read!
The quickest way to increase your vocabulary (which is the best way to improve your SAT score) is to read. If you come across a word you don't know the meaning of , look it up.

☐ Other ______________________

NOTES

9TH GRADE — WINTER TO-DO LIST

- ☐ Create a schedule so I can make sure I am allowing myself enough time to study for exams.
- ☐ Try out for seasonal activities (sports, plays, etc.).
- ☐ Meet with college counselor to plan curriculum for my sophomore, junior, and senior years.
    - ☐ Inform my college counselor if I have my heart set on going to a particular college or plan to apply to extremely competitive colleges so we can discuss fast-tracking me into honors programs.
- ☐ Other ______________________________

NOTES

9th GRADE — SPRING TO-DO LIST

- ☐ Try out for seasonal activities (sports, plays, etc.).
- ☐ Tag along when my parents take my older sister or brother to look at colleges.
- ☐ Register for my sophomore-year classes as early as possible if there is any chance they will fill up.
- ☐ Talk to my teacher, adviser, or college counselor about whether I should take the SAT II Subject Tests in math and/or biology in June (the registration deadline is in late March/April for the May test; late April/May for the June test).
    - ☐ Download the College Board's SAT Subject Test Preparation Booklet off the website, at www.collegeboard.com (free!).
    - ☐ Depending on how I do on the practice test and how important it is to me to get one of the subject tests out of the way this year, sign up for test-prep coaching service ($).
- ☐ Create a schedule so I can make sure I am allowing myself enough time to study for exams.
- ☐ Make summer plans before school gets out. (Find job or internship, enroll in camp or summer school, sign up to be a volunteer, etc.)
- ☐ Other ______________________

NOTES

9th GRADE — SUMMER TO-DO LIST

☐ Complete my 9th-grade Worksheet (see page 69) before I file away my final report card and while all of my accomplishments are still fresh in my mind.

☐ Complete my required summer reading and assignments.

☐ Do something worthwhile:

- ☐ Get a job to start putting away cash for college tuition and/or spending money.
- ☐ Get an internship in a field I want to explore.
- ☐ Volunteer for a cause I believe in.
- ☐ Go to an athletic, arts, or academic camp (or become a counselor at one).
- ☐ Go to summer school to catch up or to get ahead so I can get into honors classes sooner.

☐ Other ______________________________

Notes

9th GRADE — MAKE YOUR OWN MONTHLY TO-DO LISTS

september

- [ ]
- [ ]
- [ ]
- [ ]
- [ ]
- [ ]
- [ ]
- [ ]

october

- [ ]
- [ ]
- [ ]
- [ ]
- [ ]
- [ ]
- [ ]
- [ ]

november

- [ ]
- [ ]
- [ ]
- [ ]
- [ ]
- [ ]
- [ ]
- [ ]

december

- [ ]
- [ ]
- [ ]
- [ ]
- [ ]
- [ ]
- [ ]
- [ ]

january

- [ ]
- [ ]
- [ ]
- [ ]
- [ ]
- [ ]
- [ ]
- [ ]

february

- [ ]
- [ ]
- [ ]
- [ ]
- [ ]
- [ ]
- [ ]
- [ ]

9th Grade — make your own monthly to-do lists

march ____________________
- [ ] ____________________
- [ ] ____________________
- [ ] ____________________
- [ ] ____________________
- [ ] ____________________
- [ ] ____________________
- [ ] ____________________
- [ ] ____________________

april ____________________
- [ ] ____________________
- [ ] ____________________
- [ ] ____________________
- [ ] ____________________
- [ ] ____________________
- [ ] ____________________
- [ ] ____________________
- [ ] ____________________

may ____________________
- [ ] ____________________
- [ ] ____________________
- [ ] ____________________
- [ ] ____________________
- [ ] ____________________
- [ ] ____________________
- [ ] ____________________
- [ ] ____________________

june ____________________
- [ ] ____________________
- [ ] ____________________
- [ ] ____________________
- [ ] ____________________
- [ ] ____________________
- [ ] ____________________
- [ ] ____________________
- [ ] ____________________

july ____________________
- [ ] ____________________
- [ ] ____________________
- [ ] ____________________
- [ ] ____________________
- [ ] ____________________
- [ ] ____________________
- [ ] ____________________
- [ ] ____________________

august ____________________
- [ ] ____________________
- [ ] ____________________
- [ ] ____________________
- [ ] ____________________
- [ ] ____________________
- [ ] ____________________
- [ ] ____________________
- [ ] ____________________

10th GRADE — SCHEDULING TIPS

You're no longer the new kid on campus — and you aren't losing an hour each day trying to find your way around. But your courses seem harder. You made the varsity soccer team, which was what you wanted, but now you have even less time to get all of your work done. And socially, there's more to do than ever.

So what do you do? Same as last year . . .

plan ahead

- Make a list of all of your classes, activities, jobs, and responsibilities, then number everything in order of priority with one as the most important. Anything you get a grade in should be at the top of your list, with core classes (English, history, math, science) given the highest priority.

create a routine

- Create a weekly calendar.
- Make a daily to-do list of homework assignments and tasks. Then number them in order of importance.
- Do your homework at the same time and in the same spot each day — sitting at a table or a desk, rather than lounging on the sofa.
- Take the time to eat right.
- Stay focused on the task at hand. Things **not** to do while you are studying:
    - Watch TV.
    - Listen to music.
    - Send/receive text messages.
    - Talk on the phone.

know what to do when

- Use your study halls wisely — it's a novel idea but use this time to study rather than to goof off with friends.
- Take regular breaks—a ten-minute break each hour should be enough to recharge your battery.

Test deadlines

- Talk to your college counselor about registering for the PSAT or the PLAN at your high school.
- Take the PSAT or the PLAN (October).
- Consider taking the SAT II Subject Tests in math and/or biology. The registration deadline is in late March/April for the May test. The registration deadline is in late April/May for the June test.

the SAT subject test

The more competitive colleges require that you take three subject tests. If you don't take any this year, and you didn't take any last year, you are going to have to take three next year. On the flip side, all the colleges on your list will receive all of your SAT scores. So if you've done everything you can do to prep for it and you still think you're going to do poorly, think twice before taking it.

Notes

10th GRADE — FALL TO-DO LIST

☐ Study hard to get the best grades I can!

☐ Review my extracurricular activities — and make sure I have time to commit to my most important activities.

If applicable:

☐ Make up for being a couch potato last year! Get involved!

- ☐ Try out for sports teams.
- ☐ Join the yearbook or newspaper staff.
- ☐ Audition for the school musical.
- ☐ Run for student government.
- ☐ Other ____________________

☐ Find a cause and volunteer.

☐ Talk to my college counselor about registering for the PSAT or the PLAN at my high school.

☐ Take the PSAT or the PLAN (October).

☐ Review my PSAT or PLAN score with my college counselor — discuss ways to start preparing for the SAT or the ACT, such as reading and learning vocabulary for the SAT (put off hard-core test-prep courses until your junior year).

☐ If my verbal score on the PSAT is lower than I want it to be, read more books.

☐ Other ____________________

NOTES

10th GRADE — WINTER TO-DO LIST

- ☐ Create a schedule so I can make sure I am allowing myself enough time to study for exams.
- ☐ Try out for seasonal activities (sports, plays, etc.).
- ☐ Meet with my college counselor to reevaluate the best courses for me to take my junior year and to make sure I am still on track to becoming a good candidate for my preferred colleges.
  - ☐ Remind my college counselor if I have my heart set on going to a particular college or plan to apply to extremely competitive colleges, so we can work together to make sure I am doing everything I need to do and taking as many honors courses as I can handle.
- ☐ Other ______________________

NOTES

10th GRADE — SPRING TO-DO LIST

- ☐ Try out for seasonal activities (sports, plays, etc.).
- ☐ Tag along when my parents take my older sister or brother to look at colleges.
- ☐ Register for junior-year classes as early as possible if there is any chance they will fill up.
- ☐ Consider taking the SAT II Subject Tests in math and/or biology (the registration deadline is in late March/April for the May test; late April/May for the June test).
    - ☐ Download the College Board's SAT Subject Test Preparation Booklet off the website, at www.collegeboard.com (free!).
    - ☐ Depending on how I do on the practice test, and how important it is to me to take the subject test(s) this year, sign up for test-prep coaching service ($).
- ☐ Create a schedule to make sure I am allowing myself enough time to study for exams.
- ☐ Other ______________________

NOTES

10th GRADE — SUMMER TO-DO LIST

- ☐ Complete my 10th-grade Worksheet (see page 70) before I file away my final report card and while all of my accomplishments are still fresh in my mind.
- ☐ Complete my required summer reading and assignments.
- ☐ Convince my parents to take a detour on our family vacation so I can take a look at some colleges.
- ☐ Start searching for merit scholarships (if I intend to apply for them).
- ☐ Do something worthwhile:
  - ☐ Get a job to start/continue putting away cash for college tuition and/or spending money.
  - ☐ Get an internship in a field I want to explore.
  - ☐ Volunteer for a cause I believe in.
  - ☐ Go to an athletic, arts, or academic camp (or become a counselor at one).
  - ☐ Go to summer school to get ahead so I can get into honors classes sooner.
- ☐ Read!

Remember: The quickest way to increase your vocabulary (which is the best way to improve your SAT score) is to read. If you come across a word you don't know the meaning of, look it up.

- ☐ Other ______________________________

NOTES

10th GRADE — MAKE YOUR OWN MONTHLY TO-DO LISTS

september____________________

- [ ] ____________________
- [ ] ____________________
- [ ] ____________________
- [ ] ____________________
- [ ] ____________________
- [ ] ____________________
- [ ] ____________________
- [ ] ____________________

october____________________

- [ ] ____________________
- [ ] ____________________
- [ ] ____________________
- [ ] ____________________
- [ ] ____________________
- [ ] ____________________
- [ ] ____________________
- [ ] ____________________

november____________________

- [ ] ____________________
- [ ] ____________________
- [ ] ____________________
- [ ] ____________________
- [ ] ____________________
- [ ] ____________________
- [ ] ____________________
- [ ] ____________________

december____________________

- [ ] ____________________
- [ ] ____________________
- [ ] ____________________
- [ ] ____________________
- [ ] ____________________
- [ ] ____________________
- [ ] ____________________
- [ ] ____________________

january____________________

- [ ] ____________________
- [ ] ____________________
- [ ] ____________________
- [ ] ____________________
- [ ] ____________________
- [ ] ____________________
- [ ] ____________________
- [ ] ____________________

february____________________

- [ ] ____________________
- [ ] ____________________
- [ ] ____________________
- [ ] ____________________
- [ ] ____________________
- [ ] ____________________
- [ ] ____________________
- [ ] ____________________

10th Grade — make your own monthly to-do lists

march ______

- [ ] ______
- [ ] ______
- [ ] ______
- [ ] ______
- [ ] ______
- [ ] ______
- [ ] ______
- [ ] ______

april ______

- [ ] ______
- [ ] ______
- [ ] ______
- [ ] ______
- [ ] ______
- [ ] ______
- [ ] ______
- [ ] ______

may ______

- [ ] ______
- [ ] ______
- [ ] ______
- [ ] ______
- [ ] ______
- [ ] ______
- [ ] ______
- [ ] ______

june ______

- [ ] ______
- [ ] ______
- [ ] ______
- [ ] ______
- [ ] ______
- [ ] ______
- [ ] ______
- [ ] ______

july ______

- [ ] ______
- [ ] ______
- [ ] ______
- [ ] ______
- [ ] ______
- [ ] ______
- [ ] ______
- [ ] ______

august ______

- [ ] ______
- [ ] ______
- [ ] ______
- [ ] ______
- [ ] ______
- [ ] ______
- [ ] ______
- [ ] ______

11th GRADE — SCHEDULING TIPS

You know the drill at school. You've finally figured out how to juggle all of your classes and extracurriculars. But it seems as if your workload has tripled. Your friends are as demanding of your time as ever. And suddenly everyone wants to know where you plan to go to college — and they all seem to have an opinion about the fact that you haven't decided yet. You remind them that you're only a junior, but in your mind, you're starting to wonder how you could let such an important decision go until the last minute. Relax. Take a deep breath. You absolutely do not need to have any sort of definitive list yet. But it is time to start looking — as if you don't already have enough on your plate.

To get it all done it's more important than ever that you use the tools you have acquired to manage your time.

plan ahead

- Make a list of all of your classes, activities, jobs, and responsibilities, then number everything in order of priority with one as the most important. Anything you get a grade in should be at the top of your list, with core classes (English, history, math, science) given the highest priority.

create a routine

- Be diligent about making and prioritizing your daily to-do list of homework assignments and tasks.
- If you have a long commute to or from school or an activity, consider making a tape to help you memorize information or make flashcards to quiz yourself so you can make good use of the time.

know what to do when

- Do your homework and study when you are the most alert. The later in the evening it gets, the more your productivity drops, especially when you are tired. Staying up until three o'clock in the morning to write a paper or cram for a test does you more harm than good.

Test deadlines

☐ Register for the PSAT or the PLAN at my high school.

☐ Take the PSAT or the PLAN (October).

Register for SAT I.
Must be postmarked by ______________________
Received by ______________________

Register for ACT.
Must be postmarked by ______________________
Received by ______________________

Register for SAT Subject Test by ______________________

Remember: The more competitive colleges require that you submit three subject tests. Don't put them off until the fall for any courses you are currently taking. (You should take the test in June, when all the material is still fresh in your brain. An exception would be if you take a course in summer school, in which case the soonest test after you complete the course would be in October.)

Register for AP Exams (given in May).

☐ Call AP Services by ______________________
(888) 225-5427 (if test is not offered at my school).

☐ Call AP Coordinator to register by ______________________
(AP Services will provide the contact information if test is not offered at my school.)

NOTES

____

____

____

____

____

____

____

____

____

____

11th GRADE — FALL TO-DO LIST

- ☐ Study hard to get the best grades I can! (Grades this year count more than ever.)
- ☐ Fill out Applicant Worksheet (see pages 11–13) (if I haven't already).
- ☐ Ask my parents to fill out Parent Worksheet (see pages 15–17) (if I haven't already).
- ☐ Sit down with my parents to compare worksheets and discuss any concerns or reservations they may have (so I won't waste time applying somewhere I can't go).
- ☐ Meet with college counselor:
    - ☐ Go over my preliminary list of colleges to make sure I am on track in terms of my academics, course load, and activities to becoming a solid candidate for the colleges on my list.
    - ☐ Get suggestions from my college counselor on other schools that would be a good fit for me.
- ☐ Focus on excelling in my most important extracurricular activities.
- ☐ Take initiative and look for opportunities to excel in both my academics and extracurricular activities.
- ☐ Register for the PSAT or the PLAN at my high school.
- ☐ Take the PSAT or the PLAN (October).
- ☐ Take the practice SAT or the ACT and score myself.
- ☐ Review my most recent PSAT and practice SAT or ACT scores with my college counselor — discuss ways to start preparing for the SAT or the ACT.
- ☐ Discuss when to take the SAT or the ACT. (The SAT I test is administered in October, November, January, April, May, and June. The ACT is administered in September (limited states), October, December, February, April, and June.)
- ☐ Sign up for a test-prep course (online, classroom, or tutorial) or look into test-prep books (if necessary). (See test-prep resources on pages 64–66.)

NOTES

11th GRADE — WINTER TO-DO LIST

- ☐ Create a schedule so I can make sure I am allowing myself enough time to study for exams.
- ☐ Try out for seasonal activities (sports, plays, etc.).
- ☐ Write to colleges to get brochures.
- ☐ Focus on excelling in my most important extracurricular activities.
- ☐ Take initiative and look for opportunities to excel and take a leadership position in both my academics and extracurricular activities.
- ☐ Continue prepping for the SAT or the ACT.
- ☐ Take another SAT or ACT practice test and score myself.
- ☐ Other ____________________

NOTES

11th GRADE — SPRING TO-DO LIST

- ☐ Prep for the SAT or the ACT.
- ☐ Register for the SAT or the ACT (if I haven't already).
- ☐ Take the SAT or the ACT (if I haven't already).
- ☐ Register for AP Exams (given in May):
    - ☐ Call AP Services by ____________ (888) 225-5427 (if test is not offered at my school).
    - ☐ Call AP Coordinator to register by ____________ (AP Services will provide the contact information.) (if test is not offered at my school).
- ☐ Visit colleges over spring break.
- ☐ Meet with my college counselor to review the best courses for me to take my senior year.
- ☐ Register for senior-year classes as early as possible if there is a chance they will fill up.
- ☐ Take the required SAT II Subject Tests (the registration deadline is in late March/April for the May test; late April/May for the June test).
    - ☐ Download the College Board's *SAT Subject Test Preparation Booklet* off the Web site, at www.collegeboard.com (free!).
    - ☐ Depending on how I do on the practice test, sign up for prep-test coaching service ($).
- ☐ Create a schedule so I can make sure I am allowing myself enough time to study for exams.
- ☐ Seek out leadership positions for my senior year (student government, sports, etc.).
- ☐ Other ____________

NOTES

11th GRADE — SUMMER TO-DO LIST

- ☐ If I want to cancel my AP exam, stay on top of June 15 deadline (see page 63).
- ☐ Complete my 11th-grade worksheet before I file away my final report card and while all of my accomplishments are still fresh in my mind.
- ☐ Complete solid first draft of my application essay(s). (See essay tips on pages 109–111.)
- ☐ Complete high school resumē (see pages 73–74) if I haven't already done so.
- ☐ Fill out scholarships worksheet on pages 127–128. A large number of merit scholarship applications are due in the fall.
- ☐ Start filling out merit scholarship applications.
- ☐ Complete my required summer reading and assignments.
- ☐ Study for the SAT or the ACT (if I am taking it in the fall).
- ☐ Consider taking test-prep course (if I haven't already).
- ☐ Visit colleges I wasn't able to see in the spring and won't have time to visit in the fall (see pages 26–27).
- ☐ Do something worthwhile:
  - ☐ Get a job to start/continue putting away cash for college tuition and/or spending money.
  - ☐ Get an internship in a field I want to explore.
  - ☐ Volunteer for a cause I believe in.
  - ☐ Go to an athletic, arts, or academic camp (or become a counselor at one).
  - ☐ Go to summer school to get ahead so I can get into AP classes my senior year.
- ☐ Other ____________________

NOTES

11th GRADE — MAKE YOUR OWN MONTHLY TO-DO LISTS

september

- [ ]
- [ ]
- [ ]
- [ ]
- [ ]
- [ ]
- [ ]
- [ ]

october

- [ ]
- [ ]
- [ ]
- [ ]
- [ ]
- [ ]
- [ ]
- [ ]

november

- [ ]
- [ ]
- [ ]
- [ ]
- [ ]
- [ ]
- [ ]
- [ ]

december

- [ ]
- [ ]
- [ ]
- [ ]
- [ ]
- [ ]
- [ ]
- [ ]

january

- [ ]
- [ ]
- [ ]
- [ ]
- [ ]
- [ ]
- [ ]
- [ ]

february

- [ ]
- [ ]
- [ ]
- [ ]
- [ ]
- [ ]
- [ ]
- [ ]

11th Grade — make your own monthly to-do lists

march ____________________

- [ ] ____________________
- [ ] ____________________
- [ ] ____________________
- [ ] ____________________
- [ ] ____________________
- [ ] ____________________
- [ ] ____________________
- [ ] ____________________

april ____________________

- [ ] ____________________
- [ ] ____________________
- [ ] ____________________
- [ ] ____________________
- [ ] ____________________
- [ ] ____________________
- [ ] ____________________
- [ ] ____________________

may ____________________

- [ ] ____________________
- [ ] ____________________
- [ ] ____________________
- [ ] ____________________
- [ ] ____________________
- [ ] ____________________
- [ ] ____________________
- [ ] ____________________

june ____________________

- [ ] ____________________
- [ ] ____________________
- [ ] ____________________
- [ ] ____________________
- [ ] ____________________
- [ ] ____________________
- [ ] ____________________
- [ ] ____________________

july ____________________

- [ ] ____________________
- [ ] ____________________
- [ ] ____________________
- [ ] ____________________
- [ ] ____________________
- [ ] ____________________
- [ ] ____________________
- [ ] ____________________

august ____________________

- [ ] ____________________
- [ ] ____________________
- [ ] ____________________
- [ ] ____________________
- [ ] ____________________
- [ ] ____________________
- [ ] ____________________
- [ ] ____________________

12th GRADE — SCHEDULING TIPS

With glossy brochures stacked and piled in every corner, your bedroom looks like a clearinghouse for colleges. In addition to your academic course load, you suddenly have a lot more responsibility in your extracurricular activities, which means they take up even more of your time. And somewhere in the midst of all of this, you are expected to complete multiple applications, which require filling out multiple forms and answering multiple questions so that you seem smart and sincere but not too slick. You're a senior now.

plan ahead

- When you make a list of all of your obligations, remember to include applying to college. And don't forget to number your obligations in order of priority with one as the most important.

create a routine

- Create a weekly calendar so you can see at a glance what you need to get done and how your time is spent.
- Make a daily to-do list of homework assignments and tasks. Then number them in order of importance. Make sure the most important items on your list get the most (or best) attention.
- Take the time to eat right.
- Make sure you get enough sleep.
- Do your homework at the same time, in the same spot, each day — sitting at a table or a desk, rather than lounging on the sofa.
- Stay focused on the task at hand. Things **not** to do while you are studying:
    - Watch TV.
    - Listen to music.
    - Send/receive text messages.
    - Talk on the phone.

know what to do when

- If you have five minutes to kill, you'll have much more success memorizing a couple of vocabulary words or reading a few pages of literature for your English class (especially if you like the book) than you will tackling your precalculus homework.

12th grade — major deadlines

applications

College 1 application ______

☐ Must be postmarked by ______

☐ Received by ______

College 2 application ______

☐ Must be postmarked by ______

☐ Received by ______

College 3 application ______

☐ Must be postmarked by ______

☐ Received by ______

College 4 application ______

☐ Must be postmarked by ______

☐ Received by ______

College 5 application ______

☐ Must be postmarked by ______

☐ Received by ______

Return candidate response letter with deposit by May 1 for regular admission.

financial aid filing deadlines

CSS PROFILE Submitted online by ______
(The deadline is often as early as December 15. Be sure to check the deadlines for all of the schools on your list!)

FAFSA

☐ Must be postmarked by ______

☐ Received by ______

(The deadline usually falls between February 1 and February 15. Confirm deadlines with schools on your list.)

Other ______

☐ Must be postmarked by ______

☐ Received by ______

(Be sure to use the Financial aid worksheet (see pages 125–126) to keep track of state forms and college forms not listed here.)

test registration

Register for SAT I

☐ Must be postmarked by ______

☐ Received by ______

Register for ACT

☐ Must be postmarked by ______

☐ Received by ______

Register for SAT Subject Test by ______

Register for AP Exams by ______

scholarship deadlines

______ Application

☐ Must be postmarked by ______

☐ Received by ______

______ Application

☐ Must be postmarked by ______

☐ Received by ______

______ Application

☐ Must be postmarked by ______

☐ Received by ______

______ Application

☐ Must be postmarked by ______

☐ Received by ______

______ Application

☐ Must be postmarked by ______

☐ Received by ______

other deadlines

______

______

______

______

______

______

12th GRADE — FALL TO-DO LIST

- ☐ Study hard to get the best grades I can!
- ☐ Register for the SAT or the ACT (if I am taking it again).
- ☐ Take a SAT or an ACT practice test a couple of weeks before the exam to get back in shape (if out of practice).
- ☐ Take the SAT or the ACT.
- ☐ Meet with college counselor as early in the school year as possible:
  - ☐ Review final list of colleges to make sure my assessment of my chances of admissions at my schools is accurate.
  - ☐ Ask my college counselor to read and critique my essay.
  - ☐ Ask if I am missing any schools that he or she thinks would be a good fit for me.
- ☐ Ask teachers to write recommendations (see tips on how to get a good recommendation on page 112).
- ☐ Focus on excelling in my most important extracurricular activities.
- ☐ Take initiative and look for opportunities to excel and take a leadership role in both my academics and extracurricular activities.
- ☐ Other ______________________

NOTES

12th GRADE — WINTER TO-DO LIST

- ☐ Create a schedule so I can make sure I am allowing myself enough time to study for exams. (Unless you applied early and were accepted, colleges will receive your fall grades.)
- ☐ Complete as much as I can of my 12th-grade worksheet (see page 72) to be sure I am not leaving anything out of my applications.
- ☐ Review all of my college application checklists (on the see-through storage pockets) to confirm that I submitted all of the required documents.
- ☐ Review financial aid worksheet (see pages 125–126) to confirm that I've submitted all of the required applications to each of the schools on my list.
- ☐ Focus on excelling in my most important extracurricular activities.
- ☐ Other ______________________

NOTES

12th GRADE — SPRING TO-DO LIST

- ☐ Keep studying! Repeat five times: "I will not fall prey to senioritis, I will not fall prey to senioritis, I will not . . . ."
- ☐ Register for AP Exam(s):
  - ☐ Call AP Services by ____________ (888) 225-5427 (if test is not offered at my school).
  - ☐ Call AP Coordinator to register by ____________ (AP Services will provide the contact information.) (if test is not offered at my school).
- ☐ A soon as I hear from colleges, visit colleges I have not yet seen to help me make my decision.
- ☐ If I get waitlisted at my top choice, write the admissions officer a letter and let him or her know that I want to be kept on the list and would very much like to attend that school. Ask my college counselor to write a letter on my behalf.
- ☐ Make my final decision about where I will attend college and return the appropriate candidate response letter by May 1 (for regular admission).
- ☐ Other ____________

NOTES

12th GRADE — SUMMER TO-DO LIST

- ☐ Go to orientation weekend.
- ☐ Take a vacation!
- ☐ Get a job to save money for tuition and/or spending money for next year.
- ☐ Do something I really enjoy, or try something I've always wanted to do just for the sake of doing it (take a pottery class, volunteer).
- ☐ Other ______

NOTES

12th GRADE — MAKE YOUR OWN MONTHLY TO-DO LISTS

september________________

- ☐
- ☐
- ☐
- ☐
- ☐
- ☐
- ☐
- ☐

october________________

- ☐
- ☐
- ☐
- ☐
- ☐
- ☐
- ☐
- ☐

november________________

- ☐
- ☐
- ☐
- ☐
- ☐
- ☐
- ☐
- ☐

december________________

- ☐
- ☐
- ☐
- ☐
- ☐
- ☐
- ☐
- ☐

january________________

- ☐
- ☐
- ☐
- ☐
- ☐
- ☐
- ☐
- ☐

february________________

- ☐
- ☐
- ☐
- ☐
- ☐
- ☐
- ☐
- ☐

12th Grade — make your own monthly to-do lists

march ______________________

- [ ] ______________________
- [ ] ______________________
- [ ] ______________________
- [ ] ______________________
- [ ] ______________________
- [ ] ______________________
- [ ] ______________________
- [ ] ______________________

april ______________________

- [ ] ______________________
- [ ] ______________________
- [ ] ______________________
- [ ] ______________________
- [ ] ______________________
- [ ] ______________________
- [ ] ______________________
- [ ] ______________________

may ______________________

- [ ] ______________________
- [ ] ______________________
- [ ] ______________________
- [ ] ______________________
- [ ] ______________________
- [ ] ______________________
- [ ] ______________________
- [ ] ______________________

june ______________________

- [ ] ______________________
- [ ] ______________________
- [ ] ______________________
- [ ] ______________________
- [ ] ______________________
- [ ] ______________________
- [ ] ______________________
- [ ] ______________________

july ______________________

- [ ] ______________________
- [ ] ______________________
- [ ] ______________________
- [ ] ______________________
- [ ] ______________________
- [ ] ______________________
- [ ] ______________________
- [ ] ______________________

august ______________________

- [ ] ______________________
- [ ] ______________________
- [ ] ______________________
- [ ] ______________________
- [ ] ______________________
- [ ] ______________________
- [ ] ______________________
- [ ] ______________________

CHAPTER 4: APPLYING TO COLLEGE

Now that you know where you want to apply to college, the time has come to tackle those applications. This chapter illuminates all the different parts of the application, from the decision regarding how to apply to sample college interview questions and interview tips. Find out about the most helpful references to assist you with your essays, and learn the secrets to getting the best recommendations from your teachers. Finally, learn what to do once you hear back from colleges and what steps to take when making your final decision.

IN THIS CHAPTER

- The admissions timeline
    - ✗ Regular decision
    - ✗ Early action
    - ✗ Single-choice early action
    - ✗ Early decision
- Applications
    - ✗ Application tips
    - ✗ Application how-to manuals
    - ✗ The Common Application
    - ✗ Application resources
    - ✗ Online applications
- The essay
    - ✗ The difference between getting help and plagiarizing
    - ✗ Essay tips
    - ✗ Essay help (books and Internet)
- The short-answer questions
- Recommendations
    - ✗ Getting a good recommendation
- The interview
    - ✗ Questions an interviewer is likely to ask you
    - ✗ Interview tips
- Hearing from schools and making your final decision
    - ✗ The waitlist

THE ADMISSIONS TIMELINE

Not only do you have to decide which colleges to apply to and complete the application process for each one on your list, but you also need to decide which admissions option you will select for the colleges of your choice. The most common admissions process is regular decision, followed by three early-admission possibilities: early action, single-choice early action, and early decision. The advantage of applying early admission is that you have a better chance of being accepted. Colleges prefer applicants who want to attend their school. If you are a borderline applicant, this can mean the difference between getting in and not getting in.

Regular decision

Colleges usually send out their decisions for regular decision admissions no later than April 1. You are required to accept the admissions offer of the college of your choice in writing (using a standardized form — the candidate response letter — accompanying your acceptance letter) by May 1. You are also required to send a deposit (usually between $200 and $500) at this time.

Early action

Of the three early admission possibilities, early action is the best deal in terms of keeping your options open. You can find out in December or January whether or not a school is admitting you, but you don't have to give a response until the general candidate reply date on May 1.

There are only two reasons not to take advantage of this program: If you think your senior-year fall semester grades will be better than your junior-year grades, or if you want another shot at any of the standardized tests, you should wait to apply.

Single-choice early action

Next in preference in the early admissions category is the single-choice early action. Like standard early action, this option doesn't require you to give the school your decision until May, but unlike standard early action, the single-choice plan allows you to apply early to only one school. The most competitive schools — like Harvard, Stanford, and Yale — offer single-choice early action.

Early decision

The worst of the three in terms of keeping your options open is early decision. The reason it is the worst is that if you are admitted, you are required to attend. For this same reason, colleges are more likely to accept early-decision applicants. This is because colleges are certain that early-decision applicants want to attend and are not just applying early to get ahead of the rush. Next in terms of likelihood of acceptance is single-choice early action, with early action coming in third.

how early decision affects your financial aid package

If you are looking for financial aid, early decision can get you into some real trouble, because you are stuck with whatever financial aid the school offers you. Since you are required to withdraw your other applications, you won't have the opportunity to do any comparison-shopping in terms of financial aid packages, and you won't have any other financial aid offers with which to negotiate a better deal.

BOTTOM LINE: Unless you are absolutely certain that you want to attend a particular school and are equally certain that you will not need financial aid, apply regular decision.

NOTES

APPLICATIONS

Given that the application is the form colleges use to evaluate you as a candidate, it is astounding how often students undervalue its importance. Of course you're busy and this is just one more thing that you are trying to squeeze into an impossibly full schedule, but you do not want to risk blowing your chances of getting into the college of your dreams by not allowing enough time to fill out the application properly.

After a friend caught a typo while she was looking at one of my applications, we decided to swap and proofread all of each other's applications.

– Jenna, Memphis, Tenn.

Application tips

- Get a jump-start on the admissions process by filling in your applications and starting your essays the summer before your senior year.
- Make a copy of your application before you start, in case you make a mistake and need to start over.
- Unless your handwriting is neat and legible, type your application.
- If you make a mistake that cannot be solved with a little whiteout and a copy machine, retype or rewrite the page. Do not submit an application with words crossed out.
- Make sure you answer all the questions completely and accurately.
- Give your essay the time and energy that it deserves and demands.
- Give your short-answer questions the same careful thought and attention that you give your essay.
- If you fill out the application online, take the time to print it and proofread it before you submit it.
- Proofread, proofread, proofread your application, then proofread it again — then have a parent, a teacher, or a friend proofread it.
- Allow yourself plenty of time to get your application in by the deadline — do not put it off until the night before you need to put it in the mail.

Application how-to manuals

Acing the College Application: How to Maximize Your Chances of Admission to the College of Your Choice
Ballantine Books ($13.95)
In this book, Michele Hernãndez offers one of the few comprehensive in-depth examinations of how to use the various sections of the Common Application to best showcase your strengths. The equally exceptional essay section includes tips on what to (and not to) write about as well as parts of speech (adverbs and adjectives) and words (and) to avoid. Hernãndez goes against the grain with suggestions such as handwriting your application in blue ink so there's no question as to who filled it out. But with an 88 percent success rate in her individual college counseling business, she obviously knows a thing or two about what works, and her advice is worth seriously considering.
FINAL WORD: You get all the tips Hernãndez gives her clients, at a fraction of the cost.

Rock Hard Apps: How to Write a Killer Application
Hyperion ($16.95)
With an entire chapter devoted to the Brag Sheet, this application how-to manual by Ivywise founder Katherine Cohen, PhD, should help rid you of any inclination toward being modest when it comes time to list your achievements on your college application. Rock Hard Apps covers all of the elements of the application — grades, test scores, recommendations, the interview, extracurriculars, and of course, the essay. In the course of profiling three applicants, Cohen stresses how important it is for students to showcase themselves through their applications and not rely on their GPA and SAT scores to tell their story.
FINAL WORD: A lot of useful information, especially on how to avoid admissions pitfalls.

The Common Application

A standardized application form that is accepted at 298 colleges, the Common Application was created to cut down on the amount of time and effort college applicants spend filling out applications and writing arbitrary essays. There is no doubt that using this form streamlines the process for applicants. Students can now complete the entire process, including submitting their applications to all of their various colleges, online. Additionally, the Common Application Web site (commonapp.org) provides information on — and links to the Web sites of — the colleges that require supplemental information.

As of the 2006–2007 academic year, 73 schools, including Harvard and Yale, were using the Common Application exclusively. However, many colleges also offer their own application form, leaving students with a choice of which to use. The big concern among students, parents, and college counselors is that applicants using the Common Application to apply to these schools are not given the same consideration as candidates using the college's application. Both the creators of the Common Application and participating colleges insist that colleges do not differentiate between the two applications. To be on the safe side, if you use the Common Application, you may want to make a point of telling the admissions officer that you are genuinely interested in attending that institution.

Many schools require that you send them a supplement in addition to the Common Application. Be sure to send this material in promptly and follow up to make sure that the college received it.

Application resources

if money's no object

Application Boot Camp

www.dontworrygetin.com

Nationally renowned college admissions consultant Michele Hernãndez, in conjunction with parenting expert Mimi Doe, offers summertime College Application Boot Camp (ABC) programs in Santa Monica, Calif., and New York City, for rising seniors. Compared to her usual rates (upwards of $30,000), this four-day intensive workshop is a bargain at $9,300. As an attendee, you complete the Common Application and an admissions essay and receive coaching on interviews. In addition, Hernãndez gives you the lowdown on your chances of being admitted to the schools on your list. If you're interested, book early — ABC fills up fast.

Online applications

Many schools now offer you the option of submitting your application online. There are advantages to submitting an application online:

- You save yourself the hassle of mailing it.
- You save the college the hassle of having to input your application into a computer, since all the information is submitted digitally.
- Colleges receive the applications much faster than they would via the USPS.
- You save money on stamps.
- You save trees by cutting down on unnecessary paper.

The only real drawback to submitting an application online is that people tend to miss typos on a computer screen that they would catch on paper. If you submit your applications online, be diligent about printing them and proofreading them before you submit them.

Even if you are submitting your applications online to save trees — which is, unquestionably, a noble thing to do — be sure to print out a hard copy and store it in one of the college folders in this book.

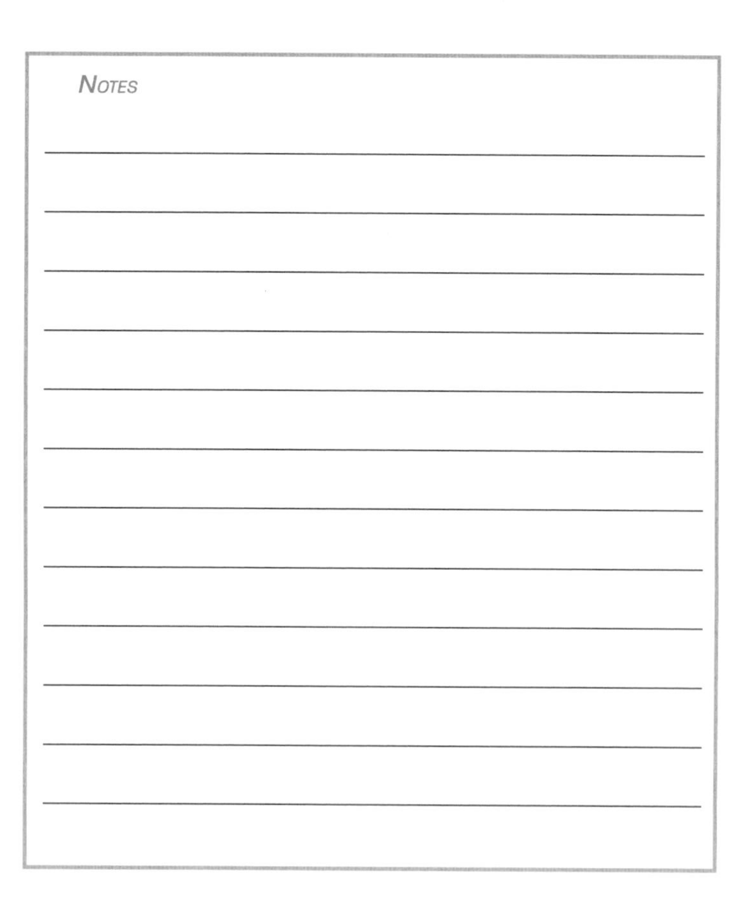

THE ESSAY

The essay is definitely one of the most nerve-racking, fear-inducing parts of the college application. As long as you use that fear to motivate you, it's a good thing. But if you become so terrified by the mere thought of having to write your essay that you slip into paralysis, then you have a problem.

Admissions officers use the essay as a tool to get to know you a little better, while simultaneously evaluating your writing ability. The best essays are those that provide admissions officers with insight into the real you, not lofty literary works that you hope to get published one day in *The New Yorker*.

The difference between getting help and plagiarizing

You have numerous resources to help you write your essay. In addition to shelves full of essay how-to manuals in bookstores and libraries, you will also find an abundance of essay help on the Web. It is okay to seek help, but be sure that when you're finished, the essay you submit is your own.

It is one thing to be provided with the tools to help you create the best possible essay; it is another thing entirely to be provided with the essay itself. There are numerous professional editing services out there. Editors should not be rewriting (or writing) your essay for you but rather offering you constructive criticism on what works and what areas need to be improved or expanded upon. (These same rules apply to parents, counselors, teachers, classmates, and friends.) Depending upon the quality of help you receive, there is no guarantee that you could not have come up with a better essay entirely on your own. So be sure that when it's all said and done, you are satisfied with the essay.

If you have any doubt about whether the help you receive on your essay is appropriate and ethical, consult a teacher, your college counselor, or your parent.

WARNING: At the risk of offending those of you who would never dream of "borrowing" someone else's essay . . .

Do not, under any circumstances, submit an essay that you did not write. Ignoring altogether the fact that doing so is completely unethical, it is a really bad idea.

Admissions officers are smart folks — and they review thousands of applications each year. They can tell pretty easily when an essay does not match the rest of an application. Furthermore, they (as well as other applicants) have access to all of the same sample essays on Web sites and in books as you do. Many schools have even started using programs that scan applicant essays and compare them to essays posted on the Web.

I saved a lot of time by reading over the essay questions on all of my applications before I got started. With a little fine-tuning, I was able to use the same essay for three different applications.

— John, Washington, D.C.

Essay tips

- Read the essay topics for each of your applications before you start to find out if, with a little fine-tuning, you can use the same essay for several applications.
- Write about something meaningful to you rather than what you think an admissions officer is going to want to read.
- Write about a specific incident or event rather than something as broad as, say, your childhood.
- Make sure your essay answers the question that is asked.
- Do not write about community service unless your experience is truly unique and shows initiative, an ongoing commitment, responsibility, and leadership.
- Do not write about your love/sex life, recreational drug and alcohol use or illegal activities.
- Avoid clichés and lofty topics.
- Have someone you trust proofread your essay for you (your college counselor, academic adviser, English teacher, parent, or sibling).

Essay help — books

50 Successful Harvard Application Essays: What Worked for Them Can Help You Get Into the College of Your Choice
St. Martin's Griffin ($12.95)
The title pretty much sums up the entire book. It is comprised of 50 essays, all from students who received that fat envelope from Harvard. Each essay is followed by an analysis from a *Harvard Crimson* staffer (Harvard's weekly newspaper). The best part about this book is the actual essays, many of which you will likely find inspiring. However, beyond the standard essay writing tips (edit, proofread, etc.), you won't find any deep insights into how to compose your own masterpiece.
FINAL WORD: Best for those looking for inspiration rather than a how-to manual.

McGraw-Hill's Writing an Outstanding College Application Essay
McGraw Hill ($13.95)
Taking its place in the workbook approach to essay writing, this book does a decent job of prompting students to write and to generate ideas using a brainstorming questionnaire. The sample essays are interesting to read, and the language is concise and clear. This approach is best for students who benefit from working out their ideas on paper. However, many students do these exercises while in class, so you may want to check with your English teacher before purchasing this book.
FINAL WORD: Good exercises if you are not already going over these topics in your English class.

Fiske Real College Essays That Work
Sourcebooks, Inc. ($14.95)
With this book, which has numerous practical tips mixed in with 109 essay samples, Fiske delivers once again. The requisite start-of-the-book advice also includes plenty of tips on pitfalls to avoid in "Five Ways to Shoot Yourself in the Foot" (melodrama is one), common typos to double-check, and when to start over. Included with each essay, sorted by category, is a concise explanation of why the essay works. The categories alone should be enough to show you the wide array of topics from which you can choose.
FINAL WORD: Practical tips and plenty of samples make this one a good buy.

Essay help — Internet

Essay Edge
www.essayedge.com
Declared "one of the best essay services on the Internet" by *The Washington Post*, Essay Edge provides top-quality feedback on admissions essays. Editing services, which will run you anywhere from $20 for proofreading an essay to $300 for walking you through the entire process, are performed by Harvard grads. If you like this service, you can use it for resumēs and medical and law school applications.
FINAL WORD: If you need essay polishing, this is the place to come.

Road To College
www.roadtocollege.com
The essay-editing services, which are provided by former admissions counselors, are among this site's more affordable offerings, at $109–$309 per essay. Other offerings on this all-around college admissions site include college counseling, SAT prep, and high school planning. But these services do not come cheap — some of Road to College's more comprehensive packages cost upwards of $1,000. For $349, Road to College even offers a mock interview and power training, performed over the phone or in person.
FINAL WORD: As former admissions officers, they know the drill.

After talking to my college counselor, I changed my topic from my spring break in Mexico, where I built a house with other members of my youth group, to my experience as captain of my lacrosse team. Even though it wasn't as exotic, it gave me a better opportunity to show my leadership skills.

— Tori, Vail, Col.

Essay help — Internet (continued)

Accepted
www.accepted.com
Concentrating on the essay portion of the college application, accepted.com is a bit pricey. The initial essay package will run you $640, or $830 for a rush job, with subsequent essays costing $480, or $625 for a rush job. You can choose the editor you wish to work with after reading the bios on the site. The first step is chatting with your editor on the phone to develop an outline for the essay. Next you swap drafts until you are satisfied. The whole shebang usually takes two weeks. The one-on-one with the editor is a good deal. The site also offers free articles, such as "Five Tips to Help You Assist Your Child With College Application Essays," which provide parents tangible advice on how to best support their teenagers as they work their way through the essay-writing process.
FINAL WORD: Need an essay? You've come to the right place.

Application Essay Writing 101 (free!)
www.collegejournal.com
If you want a free how-to manual from the founders of Essay Edge, check out Application Essay Writing 101, on the *Wall Street Journal's* College Journal Web site (www.collegejournal.com). The six lessons include everything from "Brainstorming a Topic" to "Style and Tone." If you have any doubt about how easy it is for a typo to completely alter the meaning of a sentence, check out "Actual Essay Gaffes" in lesson VI.
FINAL WORD: For do-it-yourself types, you get all the information at zero the cost.

College Essay

Get the first draft of your essay(s) out of the way over the summer.

WEEK 1 – RESEARCH

✗ **set aside 20 minutes each day for the following:**
Review the essay topics from all of your applications.

Keeping the essay questions in mind, write in a journal (any spiral notebook will work) about whatever comes to mind on the essay topics.

WEEK 2 – WRITE

✗ **choose the topic(s) for your essay(s)**
You may know exactly what you want to write about. If you don't, review your journal.

✗ **make an outline**
Using the ideas in your journal, write an outline. Do not be afraid to rearrange, combine, or alter your original thoughts.

✗ **write a first draft**
Using your outline, write your first draft. If you get stuck, reread your journal.

WEEK 3 – REVISE

✗ **revise your first draft**
Ask yourself the following questions:

Does your essay stick to the given topic?

Does it express a clear point of view?

Do you maintain a cohesive train of thought throughout your essay?

Have you checked grammar, spelling, and punctuation?

✗ **once you've finished your revisions, put your essay away until school starts**

SEPTEMBER –
Review your essay with your college counselor or a teacher. Do this within the first week of returning to school, before he or she is barraged by all of the other students.

THE SHORT-ANSWER QUESTIONS

This section of the application is not nearly as terrifying for most applicants as the essay, which unfortunately means it is often not given the necessary time and attention. Admissions officers are fully aware of the resources applicants have when it comes to writing an essay. They are also aware that students rarely utilize these same resources when answering the short-answer questions. As a result, many admissions counselors consider the short-answer questions to be a more accurate example of a student's writing ability than the essay. This is not to say that you should shortchange the essay, but rather you need to give these questions the same attention and put them through the same rigorous editing and proofreading process as you do the essay.

The short-answer questions, also sometimes known as short essays or personal statements, are often located near the essay question on a college application. Read each individual application carefully and note if the school requires specific word counts for these mini-essays or if it simply offers a paragraph count as guidance (typically one to three paragraphs).

Admissions counselors will read your short answers with an eye to how you approach the topic in question and how clearly and concisely you express your opinion. This is no place to ramble on or give endless examples. This is the place to stand out as an individual while showing off your clear thinking in a succinct answer.

Unless the application specifically requests that you write your answers directly on the application form, you should type your answers to these questions on a separate sheet or sheets (for multiple questions).

RECOMMENDATIONS

Recommendations afford admissions officers a glimpse of the person behind the grades and test scores. And it is your job to make sure they get the best look at you they possibly can. This is not a section of the application to be put off until the last minute.

Start developing relationships with your teachers early in your high school career. This will make them much more excited about writing you a recommendation — and much better able to write you a good recommendation.

Getting a good recommendation

- Choose teachers who know you well and like you — preferably teachers who are not meeting you for the first time your senior year.
- Ask — do not assume that your teacher is standing by, waiting for you to ask him or her to write you a recommendation and that asking is merely a formality — and be sure to say thank you.
- Ask in September, before he or she is barraged by everyone else in your class, who will also be seeking recommendations.

what to supply to teachers writing your recommendations

Once your teachers have agreed to write you a recommendation, give them a folder containing the following:

- A cover letter that includes:
    - A list of the information you have provided.
    - A short paragraph thanking your teacher for writing the recommendation — including why you value his or her recommendation.
    - A short paragraph letting your teacher know what you've learned from taking his or her class.
    - A short paragraph outlining things that you would like mentioned in the recommendation. (Again, ask; don't tell. Nobody — least of all your teacher — wants to feel like a puppet.)
- The recommendation form.
- Your high school resumē (See the student resumē on pages 73–74.)
- Noteworthy papers/projects — especially ones that were assigned by that teacher.
- Letters of commendation.
- The list of schools where you are applying, with deadlines noted for each school.
- Preaddressed, stamped envelopes for each of the schools on your list.

Get Into Any College: Secrets of Harvard Students
SuperCollege ($16.95)
This book, written by college admissions experts and media darlings Gene and Kelly Tanabe, should definitely be on your required reading list. The section on how to go about getting a recommendation from teachers is reason alone to purchase the book. They urge you to make a copy of the article, "Evaluating the Evaluation," which you'll find in their book, and hand it to your teachers to help them write the best possible recommendation for you. Other highlights from this book include the essay section. In addition to including samples of essays that didn't make the grade, complete with an explanation as to why, the book also lists topics to avoid, such as sex, bad grades, drugs and alcohol, and getting in trouble or arrested. Plus, there are practical tips on how to fill out your applications.
FINAL WORD: This admissions manual has great tips on getting a recommendation and writing the essay.

NOTES

THE INTERVIEW

Most of the questions you will be asked will pertain directly to the college, to you, and to your life experience. It is important that you read up on the college and don't walk into the interview blind. However, you should absolutely resist the temptation to embellish your answers. All it takes is one follow-up question for the interviewer to realize that your previous answer may not have been entirely truthful.

At some point the conversation will turn to your family. This is not the time for sarcasm, to air dirty laundry, or to inform the interviewer that your overachieving parent is forcing you to apply to the college so that he or she can live vicariously through you. Focus on the positive aspects of your family life and leave the rest for family counseling.

Above all, get a good night's sleep before the interview so you are well rested and able to converse intelligently with your interviewer. If you are nervous, ask a parent, teacher, college counselor, or friend to do a mock interview with you.

Questions an interviewer is likely to ask you

- What are your favorite/least favorite classes?
- What can you tell me about yourself?
- What can you tell me about your family?
- What do you think of (fill in the blank with the most recent national or world event)?
- What do you want to do when you grow up?
- What do you want to study in college?
- What has been your favorite/least favorite thing about high school?
- What will you contribute to our school?
- What's the last book you read?
- Why do you want to attend this school?

BE AWARE: At some of the more competitive colleges, interviewers will ask you questions designed to knock you off balance so they can see how you respond under pressure. This is just an annoying little game that they play. Do not let this type of question get you flustered. Saying that you don't know the answer is much better than giving the wrong answer or panicking.

Interview tips

Like your recommendations and essay, the interview is an opportunity for the college to get to know who you are as a person, beyond the piece of paper that contains your name and vitals (in this case, your GPA and test scores).

The interview is not and should not be a one-sided process. Treat the interview as your opportunity to get information about the college. With the exception of the most competitive colleges, many schools offer interviews for informational purposes only.

- Dress appropriately — absolutely no jeans, midriffs, T-shirts, shorts, etc.
- Arrive on time.
- Look the interviewer in the eye when you shake his or her hand.
- Learn about the person you are talking to — the information you receive and the questions you ask will be different depending on whether you are speaking with an alum or someone from the admissions office.
- Be yourself — do not try to be someone you think the interviewer wants you to be. The interviewer wants to know who you are.
- Ask smart questions (avoid obvious questions that you can answer, and should have already answered, for yourself by visiting the college's Web site or by picking up a college guide).
- Listen to and be interested in what the interviewer is saying. Connect with the interviewer on a personal level by asking questions about his or her experiences at the college (classes/major, extracurriculars, dorms, town/city).
- Answer questions thoughtfully and honestly — you are not expected to know everything, so if you don't know the answer to a question, it's perfectly okay to admit it.
- Don't be boastful, but be sure to tell the interviewer about your accomplishments when he or she asks.
- Be sure to thank the interviewer for taking the time to meet with you.

WHAT TO AVOID: Avoid the same topics in your college interviews that you avoid in your college essay — do not discuss your love/sex life, recreational drug and alcohol use, illegal activities, or anything else that is likely to reflect poorly on you or make your interviewer uncomfortable.

I wanted to throw up I was so nervous about my interview with [my first-choice college]. I found out after it was over that it didn't even count — it was just so I could learn about the school.

— Greg, Fort Worth, Tex.

NOTES

HEARING FROM SCHOOLS AND MAKING YOUR FINAL DECISION

Hopefully, you were accepted at all of your schools, you have a clear first choice, and you have plenty of money to cover the tuition, or your financial aid package is sufficient to cover it. If so, congratulations!

If things are not falling into place quite so neatly, do not worry. A good number of applicants have some hurdle to overcome once the college letters start rolling in. For some people, it is not getting into the school of their dreams. For others, it is getting in but not being able to afford the tuition. (If you are having issues with financial aid, check out the chapter on Applying for Financial Aid for tips on how to negotiate with schools to get more aid.) For others still, it is not knowing which school to choose. And of course, there is the possibility of being stuck in the uncertainty of being waitlisted.

If you have not visited all of the schools you are considering, now is the time to do it. (No matter how busy you are, or how inconvenient it is, it is really important that you make time to visit each school before sending in your deposit and telling a school you will attend. Colleges rarely look just the way they do in the brochure.)

I had it in my mind that I wanted to go to [a certain school] because I liked what I read about it on the Web site, but when I finally visited in April, I hated everything about it.

— Bree, Wilmington, Del.

The waitlist

While being waitlisted is considered by many to be better than being flat-out rejected, it can be equally frustrating since it only prolongs an already drawn-out process. And more often than not, waitlisted students don't in.

If you've been waitlisted by a college and you still want to attend, be sure to:

- Submit any requested documents — and double-check to make sure your admissions file is complete.
- Write the admissions officer a letter telling him or her that you would like to remain on the waitlist and you are still very excited about the prospect of attending that school. Also, be sure to mention any noteworthy awards or grades you have received or projects you have taken on since submitting your application.
- Ask your college counselor if he or she would be willing to write the school a letter asserting that you would be an asset to that school.

Once you've done everything you can do to help your chances of getting off the waitlist, go ahead and decide which school, among those that have accepted you, you would like to attend. Be sure to send in your candidate response letter and deposit by May 1. Do not wait to hear from your waitlisted school. If you miss the deadline at the other colleges and you do not get off the waitlist, you could wind up with nowhere to go in the fall. With few exceptions, your odds of getting off the waitlist are not great. So by all means, hope for the best, but go on about your life and start getting excited about another school.

If you are one of the lucky few to get accepted off the waitlist, congratulations! As soon as you let that school know you will be attending, be sure to notify the other school as soon as possible that you have decided to go elsewhere.

NOTES

CHAPTER 5: APPLYING FOR FINANCIAL AID

As if applying to college isn't daunting enough, if you're like many applicants, you also have to figure out how you're going to pay for it. For the 99.9 percent of you who will not qualify for a national merit scholarship or be given a free ride because of your unparalleled athletic prowess, there is still hope. This section will cover the financial aid options out there and how to go about applying for them.

IN THIS CHAPTER

- An overview of financial aid
  - Grants
  - Federal work study
  - Scholarships
  - Loans
  - Tax breaks
- How to apply for financial aid
  - The FAFSA
  - College Scholarship Service Financial Aid (CSS Profile)
  - Extenuating circumstances
- The financial aid package
  - Negotiating for more aid
  - Financial aid worksheet
  - Grants and scholarships worksheet

AN OVERVIEW OF FINANCIAL AID

Applying for financial aid can be a tedious process. It is more time-consuming and laborious than anything else. But if receiving financial aid means the difference between attending and not attending the college of your dreams, then it is unquestionably worth the effort. Hang in there!

There are three major types of financial aid: grants, scholarships, and loans. In a nutshell, grants and scholarships are preferable to loans, since they constitute free money to be used toward your tuition — and they are tax-free. It should come as no big surprise that because of this, they are much harder to get.

Depending on your family's financial situation, you will be applying for one of two types of aid: merit- or need-based.

merit-based aid

This type of financial aid is reserved for students who exhibit the greatest talent, usually in the field of academics, arts, athletics, leadership, or music. A student's financial need is not factored into merit-based aid.

need-based aid

This is given to students with the greatest financial need — in other words, the ones with the least money. With the exception of certain types of federal aid, a student's "merit" is inevitably factored into many types of need-based aid since colleges have limited funds to go around. And it doesn't take a rocket scientist to figure out that colleges prefer to give their money to students at the top of their applicant pool rather than to students at the bottom.

The best ways to learn about financial aid options are as follows:

- Talk to your financial adviser.
- Talk to your college counselor.
- Check out free Web sites and search engines such as collegeanswer.com and scholarshipexperts.com.
- Read books dedicated to scholarships and financial aid.
- Talk to the financial aid officers at the colleges on your list.

if you want to get straight up answers about financial aid on the Web, check out . . .

www.collegeanswer.com

A *Forbes* "Best of the Web" pick, this site, — funded by the leading education lending institution in the United States, Sallie Mae — is chock-full of tips on how to pay for a college education. You'll find valuable information on topics such as potential requirements for scholarships, test dates, and other deadlines. You have immediate access to Scholarship Experts search engine, online applications through College Net, and a school search directory and test-prep information by Peterson's. You'll also find financial advice on tax benefits, and loan and grant information, among other topics. The page on scholarship scams is definitely worth a read.

NOTES

Grants

Federal grants, which go to the students with the greatest financial need, fall under need-based aid. (There are numerous other types of grants that most commonly benefit underrepresented minorities, often in specific fields. You can search for these grants through one of the free scholarship search engines.) There are two main types of federal grants:

federal pell grant

This is a financial award, of up to $4,050 annually, for undergraduates with financial need. The government provides schools with the funds to award all eligible students with the maximum amount of money that each student qualifies for. Since this is a grant as opposed to a loan, it does not have to be repaid.

federal supplemental education opportunity grant (FSEOG)

This is a financial award, of $100 to $4,000 annually, given to students with the greatest financial need, with Pell Grant recipients given priority. Unlike the Pell Grant, which is promised to everyone who qualifies for it, there is no guarantee that a student with financial need will receive the FSEOG. Whether a student receives the grant and the amount awarded depend on the level of available funds from individual colleges.

Federal work study

This isn't a grant, but it is a federal program that provides jobs (usually on campus) for qualifying students with proven financial need in exchange for tuition. (If you are participating in this program, be sure to secure your job as early as possible.)

Scholarships

Scholarships, as opposed to grants, usually fall into the category of merit-based awards or a combination of merit- and need-based awards. You may be eligible for a number of scholarships based on a variety of criteria — they aren't just for intellectual giants and sports superstars.
Scholarships can come from a variety of sources

- Colleges
- Large corporations (Coca-Cola for one)
- Employers
- Individual benefactors
- Religious organizations
- Professional associations and organizations

scholarship search engines and books

It seems as if there must be at least 1,001 Web sites and search engines devoted to scholarships. (If you're curious, Google scholarships and you will see just how many sites are out there.)

Almost all of the search engines claim that they can direct you to millions of dollars in unclaimed scholarships. Some even guarantee you a scholarship, provided you pay to sign up for their service. (Any sort of guarantee is a huge red flag!) It is important to note: The best Web sites and search engines are free! One such site is www.scholarshipexperts.com.

There are a vast number of excellent scholarships out there, and more than a few legitimate search engines. But you need to use common sense to avoid unscrupulous companies that want to take your money, instead of helping you find money. So definitely search, but search wisely.

> If I were to add up all the time I wasted searching for $100 scholarships, I probably would've been better off working for minimum wage at [a fast-food chain].
>
> — Cliff, Santa Barbara, Calif., whose parents ultimately took out a PLUS Loan

save your money! think twice before using scholarship search engines that require payment.

Scholarship Experts
www.scholarshipexperts.com (free!)
Endorsed by *Forbes*, *CNN Money*, Kaplan, and Yahoo Education (and it's the search engine used by Sallie Mae's College Answer Web site), this search engine is phenomenal. You can use a variety of filters — academics, extracurriculars, hobbies — to narrow down the 2.4 million scholarships in the site's database to a manageable list of likely matches. You can also download scholarship applications directly off the site. Not only is Scholarship Experts free, but it also won't sell your information, unlike some of the other less scrupulous sites out there.

scholarship scams: buyer, beware!

Following are some telltale signs of a scholarship scam:

- Asking for your credit card or bank account information.
- Claiming that the site has exclusive scholarship information that no one else can provide.
- Demanding monthly payments.
- Giving you a hard sell, with comments such as "Act now or lose out . . . ."
- Informing you that you are a finalist for a competition you didn't enter.
- Offering a money-back guarantee.
- Offering a scholarship guarantee.

For more information on how to avoid falling prey to scholarship scams, go to www.collegeanswer.com, type "scholarship scams" in the upper right-hand corner. You can also obtain information on this site about how to report scholarship fraud.

Give your scholarship applications the same careful attention that you give to your college applications. Make sure you answer all of the questions. And proofread your application thoroughly before submitting it.

WARNING: Do NOT give your credit or bank information to any scholarship-search company unless you are absolutely certain that the company is legitimate. And think twice before providing personal information on scholarship search Web sites — unscrupulous companies can use such information to steal your identity.

Loans

Unlike grants and scholarships, loans have to be repaid — with interest. The one good thing about an education loan is you get a better interest rate than you would on many other types of loans. Also, need-based student loans are usually subsidized (at least in part) by the government, which means you do not owe any interest on the loan until you graduate or fall below half-time student status.

loan programs

There are essentially two types of loan programs: the direct loan (DL) program and the Federal Family Education Loan (FFEL) Program. With direct loans, the funds are loaned to you directly by the government. With an FFEL loan, private lenders, such as banks, provide the funds.

types of loans

There are a few types of education loans. Following is a brief description of each. You are strongly urged to consult a financial adviser to find the type of loan that will best suit your needs and those of your family.

I would've done better if I'd given myself more time to complete my scholarship applications. I had no idea I would have to write yet another essay. I stayed up until 2 AM trying to get it done . . . I didn't get the scholarship.

— Clancy, Falls Church, Va.

PLUS loan (parent loan for undergraduate students)

This is a federal loan your parents can take out to help pay for your education. It is based on your parents' credit history, rather than financial need. PLUS Loans can be obtained through the FFEL or Direct Loan Program.

With a PLUS Loan, your parents cannot borrow more than the amount of tuition they actually have to pay. What this means is that any financial aid you receive will be deducted from the total tuition cost. The resulting number is the maximum amount they can borrow. PLUS loans have a maximum interest rate of 9 percent. There is also a loan fee of 4 percent that is automatically deducted from each payment. Your parents do not have to start repaying the loan until 60 days after they receive their final disbursement.

stafford loan

This is a federal student loan, which is available through the FFEL Program and the Direct Loan Program. There are subsidized and unsubsidized Stafford Loans. The amount you can borrow ranges from $2,625 to $10,500. How much you can borrow and whether or not you qualify for a subsidized loan depend on several factors: (1) whether your parents claim you as a dependent, (2) whether you have financial need, and (3) what year you are in college. This loan has a variable interest rate, capped at 8.25 percent. The repayment period, which commences six months after you graduate or fall below half-time student status, is ten years. There is a 4 percent loan fee, which is automatically deducted from each loan payment.

perkins loan

This type of loan is reserved for students with the lowest expected family contribution. Although this is a federal loan, it is offered and repaid through your school. There is no guarantee that eligible students will receive a Perkins Loan. The number of students who receive it and the amount of each loan are based on the level of available funds from individual colleges. The repayment period, which commences nine months after you graduate or fall below half-time student status, is ten years. The maximum loan amount is $4,000 per year. The interest rate is 5 percent. There is no loan fee for a Perkins Loan.

Tax breaks

When it comes time to pay for college, the federal government will cut you (whoever can claim the student as a dependent) some slack in the form of tax credits and tax-free savings accounts. (You must qualify for the tax credits, so be sure to read the fine print.)

hope tax credit

This is an annual tax credit of up to $1,500 per student for first- and second-year college students. You cannot claim this and the Lifetime Learning Credit in the same year. You do not qualify if you make more than $53,000 per year, or $107,000 if you file a joint return.

lifetime learning credit

This is an annual tax credit of up to $2,000 that you can use to offset the costs of your college tuition. You cannot claim this and the Hope Tax Credit in the same year. You do not qualify if you make more than $53,000 per year, or $107,000 if you file a joint return.

For more information on these and other tax benefits, call the IRS at (800) 829-1040 or visit the Web site at www.irs.gov, where you can get a copy of Tax Benefits for Higher Education (IRS Publication 970).

529 savings plan

This is a state-run education savings plan that provides certain tax benefits. The types of plans, benefits, and requirements vary from state to state. This is definitely one to talk through with your financial adviser, since the type of plan you choose can have a big impact on the contribution your family is expected to make.

HOW TO APPLY FOR FINANCIAL AID

Now that you are up to speed on the various types of financial aid, you may be wondering how to go about getting this aid.

The one form that is universally required if you want financial aid is the Free Application for Federal Aid (FAFSA). However, this may not be the first form that you fill out. Many schools also require the College Scholarship Service Financial Aid PROFILE (CSS PROFILE). The CSS PROFILE can be submitted in the fall (unlike the FAFSA, which cannot be filed until after January 1) and is usually due much earlier than the FAFSA. Some schools also use state forms, as well as their own forms. Check with the admissions office at each of the schools on your list to find out individual requirements and deadlines. You can enter all of this information on the Financial Aid Worksheet at the end of this chapter so that you will have everything on one sheet, in one easy-to-reference place.

THE FAFSA

what is it?

The FAFSA is the form the federal government uses to determine how much federal financial aid you qualify for, based on the financial information you provide. The federal government shares this information with the colleges you list on the form. These institutions factor this information into their decision on how much aid they are going to give you.

when do you file it?

The earliest you can submit the FAFSA is January 1. The deadline varies, but to be safe, get it in before February 1. Ideally, you should submit it as soon after January 1 as possible. (However, as far as the government is concerned, the actual deadline is not until June 1.)

If you submit the FAFSA via snail mail, it can take up to a month to get your results. If you submit it online, it can take as little as a week. Another bonus to filling it out online is that you get immediate feedback if you enter any information incorrectly.

don't you need to have your taxes done first?

No. Contrary to popular belief, you (or your parents) do not need to have filed your taxes to submit the FAFSA. You do, however, need to have an estimate of the numbers you (or your parents) will be entering on your tax forms. Once you file your taxes, you (or your parents) can submit any revisions you need to make to the FAFSA.

how do you fill it out?

You can fill it out on the Web site at www.fafsa.ed.gov/ and submit it online, or download the form from the Web site and fill it out by hand.

Be sure to make a copy (or print a hard copy if you filled it out online) and store it in your financial aid folder. You should also make copies of all of your financial documents and tax paperwork and those of your parents. Colleges may ask you to submit these documents for verification. And even if they don't, you should hold onto this paperwork, as it will make your life infinitely easier when it comes time to reapply next year.

If you get stuck while filling out this form and want some help, go to www.studentaid.ed.gov or call the Federal Student Aid Information Center at 1-800-4-FED-AID (800-433-3243).

what happens next?

You receive your Student Aid Report (SAR), which contains your expected family contribution (EFC). You subtract your EFC from the cost of your tuition to determine your financial need.

College Scholarship Service Financial Aid (CSS PROFILE)

what is it?

The CSS PROFILE is a form many colleges use, in conjunction with the FAFSA, to determine the amount of financial aid the school will provide the student, in the form of loans, grants, and/or scholarships.

The way your financial need is evaluated on the CSS PROFILE is more complex than it is on the FAFSA. The colleges on your list dictate which questions you will have to answer on your CSS PROFILE. Home equity can be considered an asset on the CSS PROFILE, as well as life insurance policies, pension plans, and retirement funds. Further, the CSS PROFILE factors in the assets of a noncustodial parent, while the FAFSA does not. Unless you have numerous siblings attending private school, which actually counts in your favor on the CSS PROFILE, your expected family contribution is likely to be higher on the CSS PROFILE than it would be according to the FAFSA.

There is also a $5 registration fee, plus $18 per school receiving the CSS PROFILE.

when do you file it?

The earliest you can register for the CSS PROFILE is October 1. The deadlines range from December 15 through February 1, depending on the school.

how do you register for it?

You must fill out and submit the CSS PROFILE online by going to www.collegeboard.net. Before you submit the CSS PROFILE, be sure to print a hard copy and file it in your financial aid folder.

what happens next?

You cross your fingers and wait to see what sort of financial aid package colleges will offer you.

Extenuating circumstances

Be sure to notify the financial aid officer at the colleges on your list of any extenuating circumstances that may affect your or your parents' ability to meet your expected family contribution.

A parent's being laid off, medical bills, and siblings enrolled in college are all factors that colleges will take into consideration when evaluating your financial need.

THE FINANCIAL AID PACKAGE

This is the combination of grants, scholarships, and loans that a student receives from colleges. (Generally speaking more than 50 percent of the package consists of loans rather than grants and scholarships.)

Hopefully, you got accepted by your first-choice college, and the school is providing you with all of the money you need. (It has happened!) If this isn't your situation, and your first-choice school did not provide you with a big enough financial aid package, don't despair. There may still be hope.

Negotiating for more aid

It's time to start bargaining.

Many schools will tell you that their financial aid package is nonnegotiable. This isn't entirely true. But the last thing you want to do is upset the school that you would like to attend, so approach this situation wisely. You will get a lot farther by being polite and asking the financial aid office to reconsider your financial aid package than by demanding that the college just give you the money you so obviously deserve.

The best thing to do is to write a letter addressed to the financial aid officer, explaining your circumstances and why the college's package does not meet your financial need. Elaborate on any of the following that apply to make the case that you need and deserve more aid:

- Extenuating circumstances (siblings in college, a parent laid off).
- You received a better financial aid package from another college.
- Your financial aid package was significantly less than their average financial aid package. (You can find out the size of a school's average financial aid package by going to www.collegeboard.com. Enter the school name in the College QuickFinder box, then click on Cost and Financial Aid.)

TIP: Hopefully, you applied to and were accepted by at least one safety school, which should have offered you an impressive financial aid package, since you were at the top of the applicant pool. With a better deal in hand, you have more leverage in negotiating for additional financial aid from another school.

Financial Aid Resources

Fastweb (free!)
www.fastweb.com
In existence since 1995, Fastweb was one of the first college scholarship search engines created, and it is still one of the most commonly used sites today. You will find information on college, local, and national scholarships. And Fastweb will match you with scholarships that best suit your qualifications. The site also offers information on colleges, jobs, and internships for students.
FINAL WORD: If you're looking for a scholarship clearing house, this is a good place to go.

How to Go to College Almost for Free
Collins ($22)
If you're looking for tips from a pro, you won't do any better than this book by Ben Kaplan, who was awarded $90,000 in scholarship money to attend Harvard. In addition to inspiring awe among readers, Kaplan delivers easy-to-follow advice on how to find and apply for scholarships, covering such topics as the essay, the interview, and getting the best possible recommendations.
FINAL WORD: This should be required reading for financial aid applicants.

The Complete Idiot's Guide to Financial Aid for College
Alpha ($18.95)
Covering everything from tax laws to student loans to where to find scholarship and grant money, this user-friendly book gives a solid overview of the process of finding and applying for financial aid. It includes the FAFSA and CSS PROFILE forms, shows you how to fill them out, and tells you what type of information to include on each form. This guide also includes tips on how to make yourself a good candidate for financial aid and how to negotiate for a better financial aid package. More than a few students swear by the directory in the back of this book.
FINAL WORD: If you're looking to have your hand held all the way through the process, this is the book for you.

Paying for College Without Going Broke
The Princeton Review ($20)
Thorough, up-to-date, and comprehensive, this book is a good buy if you're serious about searching for financial aid. It takes you step by step through the entire process. It includes the latest financial aid forms with instructions on filling them out. And the easy to follow explanation of the tax laws is updated annually. You'll also find tips on what you can do to make yourself eligible for aid (or more aid).
FINAL WORD: A good buy.

The Scholarship Scouting Report: An Insider's Guide to America's Best Scholarships
Collins ($22.95)
Those of you who are tired of searching on Fastweb and other Internet search engines will appreciate this book by Ben Kaplan, the poster child for getting financial aid (see *How to Go to College Almost for Free*). The scholarships profiled in this book are those available to the largest pool of people (need- and region-based scholarships are not included). Although at times a bit goofy, with a lot of graphics and photos of scholarship winners, this book is a good one if you are scouting for scholarships.
FINAL WORD: A good place to start your search.

The Sports Scholarships Insider's Guide: Getting Money for College at Any Division
Sourcebooks ($16.95)
This book is a must have for every student athlete who thinks he or she may want to play a sport in college — and get a free ride to do so. Covering topics like negotiating tips, the recruitment process, and constructing a profile, this clear and concise book does a good job of taking you through the recruitment process.
FINAL WORD: Athletes, pick one up.

FINANCIAL AID WORKSHEET

Use the following checklists to keep track of the required forms, when they're due, and whether you've submitted them. Both the FAFSA and the CSS PROFILE are automatically sent to the schools that you list on the respective applications, so be sure not to omit any. Be sure to review the requirements carefully for each of the schools on your list.

college 1 ______________________

required	form	deadline	submitted
☐	**FAFSA**	________	☐
☐	**CSS PROFILE**	________	☐
☐	**STATE FORM**	________	☐
☐	**COLLEGE FORM**	________	☐
☐	**OTHER** ________	________	☐

FA officer ______________________

Phone ______________________

E-mail ______________________

Notes ______________________

____

college 2 ______________________

required	form	deadline	submitted
☐	**FAFSA**	________	☐
☐	**CSS PROFILE**	________	☐
☐	**STATE FORM**	________	☐
☐	**COLLEGE FORM**	________	☐
☐	**OTHER** ________	________	☐

FA officer ______________________

Phone ______________________

E-mail ______________________

Notes ______________________

____

college 3 ______________________

required	form	deadline	submitted
☐	**FAFSA**	________	☐
☐	**CSS PROFILE**	________	☐
☐	**STATE FORM**	________	☐
☐	**COLLEGE FORM**	________	☐
☐	**OTHER** ________	________	☐

FA officer ______________________

Phone ______________________

E-mail ______________________

Notes ______________________

____

college 4 ______________________

required	form	deadline	submitted
☐	**FAFSA**	________	☐
☐	**CSS PROFILE**	________	☐
☐	**STATE FORM**	________	☐
☐	**COLLEGE FORM**	________	☐
☐	**OTHER** ________	________	☐

FA officer ______________________

Phone ______________________

E-mail ______________________

Notes ______________________

____

FINANCIAL AID WORKSHEET

college 5 ______________________

required	form	deadline	submitted
☐	**FAFSA**	________	☐
☐	**CSS PROFILE**	________	☐
☐	**STATE FORM**	________	☐
☐	**COLLEGE FORM**	________	☐
☐	**OTHER** ________	________	☐

FA officer ______________________

Phone ______________________

E-mail ______________________

Notes ______________________

____

college 6 ______________________

required	form	deadline	submitted
☐	**FAFSA**	________	☐
☐	**CSS PROFILE**	________	☐
☐	**STATE FORM**	________	☐
☐	**COLLEGE FORM**	________	☐
☐	**OTHER** ________	________	☐

FA officer ______________________

Phone ______________________

E-mail ______________________

Notes ______________________

____

college 7 ______________________

required	form	deadline	submitted
☐	**FAFSA**	________	☐
☐	**CSS PROFILE**	________	☐
☐	**STATE FORM**	________	☐
☐	**COLLEGE FORM**	________	☐
☐	**OTHER** ________	________	☐

FA officer ______________________

Phone ______________________

E-mail ______________________

Notes ______________________

____

college 8 ______________________

required	form	deadline	submitted
☐	**FAFSA**	________	☐
☐	**CSS PROFILE**	________	☐
☐	**STATE FORM**	________	☐
☐	**COLLEGE FORM**	________	☐
☐	**OTHER** ________	________	☐

FA officer ______________________

Phone ______________________

E-mail ______________________

Notes ______________________

____

GRANTS AND SCHOLARSHIPS WORKSHEET

Use this worksheet to keep track of all of your scholarship applications, requirements, and deadlines.

award name ______________________________

____

- ☐ Application Deadline ______________
- ☐ Application
- ☐ Questions
- ☐ Recommendations
- ☐ Transcript
- ☐ Other ______________

Notes ______________________________

____

award name ______________________________

____

- ☐ Application Deadline ______________
- ☐ Application
- ☐ Questions
- ☐ Recommendations
- ☐ Transcript
- ☐ Other ______________

Notes ______________________________

____

award name ______________________________

____

- ☐ Application Deadline ______________
- ☐ Application
- ☐ Questions
- ☐ Recommendations
- ☐ Transcript
- ☐ Other ______________

Notes ______________________________

____

award name ______________________________

____

- ☐ Application Deadline ______________
- ☐ Application
- ☐ Questions
- ☐ Recommendations
- ☐ Transcript
- ☐ Other ______________

Notes ______________________________

____

award name ______________________________

____

- ☐ Application Deadline ______________
- ☐ Application
- ☐ Questions
- ☐ Recommendations
- ☐ Transcript
- ☐ Other ______________

Notes ______________________________

____

award name ______________________________

____

- ☐ Application Deadline ______________
- ☐ Application
- ☐ Questions
- ☐ Recommendations
- ☐ Transcript
- ☐ Other ______________

Notes ______________________________

____

GRANTS AND SCHOLARSHIPS WORKSHEET

award name ____________________

- ☐ Application Deadline ____________
- ☐ Application
- ☐ Questions
- ☐ Recommendations
- ☐ Transcript
- ☐ Other ____________

Notes ____________________

award name ____________________

- ☐ Application Deadline ____________
- ☐ Application
- ☐ Questions
- ☐ Recommendations
- ☐ Transcript
- ☐ Other ____________

Notes ____________________

award name ____________________

- ☐ Application Deadline ____________
- ☐ Application
- ☐ Questions
- ☐ Recommendations
- ☐ Transcript
- ☐ Other ____________

Notes ____________________

award name ____________________

- ☐ Application Deadline ____________
- ☐ Application
- ☐ Questions
- ☐ Recommendations
- ☐ Transcript
- ☐ Other ____________

Notes ____________________

award name ____________________

- ☐ Application Deadline ____________
- ☐ Application
- ☐ Questions
- ☐ Recommendations
- ☐ Transcript
- ☐ Other ____________

Notes ____________________

award name ____________________

- ☐ Application Deadline ____________
- ☐ Application
- ☐ Questions
- ☐ Recommendations
- ☐ Transcript
- ☐ Other ____________

Notes ____________________

QUICK REFERENCE SHEET

Admissions

college search engines

www.collegeboard.com (free!)*
www.petersons.com (free!)*
www.princetonreview.com (free!)*

information

www.collegeconfidential.com (free!)*

Test prep

www.collegeboard.com (free!)*
www.kaplan.com
www.number2.com (free!)
www.prepme.com
www.princetonreview.com

Financial aid

information

www.studentaid.ed.gov (free!)
www.collegeanswer.com (free!)
www.collegeparents.org (free!)

forms

www.fafsa.ed.gov (Free Application for Federal Aid) (free!)
www.collegeboard.net (CSS PROFILE) (free!)

scholarship search engine

www.scholarshipexperts.com (free!)

There are other services on this site that are not free.

NOTES

GLOSSARY

ACT This is a college entrance exam that is similar to the SAT. It's more popular in the Midwest and the South. Students who get good grades but don't do well on standardized tests sometimes score higher on the ACT than they do on the SAT. A perfect score on the ACT is 36.
WHAT IT MEANS TO YOU: Depending on how well you test, where you're applying, and how motivated you are, you may want or need to take the ACT. You can always take both tests and decide which to submit.

Advanced Placement (AP) Courses AP courses are college-level courses offered in high school. Upon passing the AP exam, students can receive a college credit. AP courses carry a heavier weight than regular courses, allowing AP students to exceed a 4.0 GPA.
WHAT IT MEANS TO YOU: If you can hack them, take them. Colleges look very favorably on AP courses, provided you do well in them.

Advanced Placement (AP) Exams AP Exams are held every May across the country. The exams are scored from 1 to 5. Most universities will accept a score of 3 or better for college credit.
WHAT IT MEANS TO YOU: Since the test is in May, your coursework will end way before school does! You also get a head start on your college course load.

College Board This is the organization that everyone has to thank for the SAT I and II. The College Board also runs the PSAT and the AP programs, publishes several college admissions manuals and guidebooks, and administers the CSS PROFILE.
WHAT IT MEANS TO YOU: This organization runs your life your junior and senior year.

Common Application A universal application that is accepted at nearly 300 universities, this form saves you from spending hours filling out individual applications. *(For more information, see the Common Application on page 108.)*
WHAT IT MEANS TO YOU: Less work. But check the colleges on your list to see if they require any supplemental information.

CSS PROFILE Administered by the College Board, the CSS PROFILE is a form you fill out that colleges use to determine the amount of financial aid you need. It is similar to the FAFSA, with the following exceptions: It takes more factors into consideration in evaluating your assets. The colleges dictate the questions you must answer. It can be submitted in the fall. It costs $5–$18 per school.
WHAT IT MEANS TO YOU: More paperwork. But if you're looking for financial aid, you don't have a choice.

FYI

In case you're wondering what all those acronyms stand for

ACT	American College Testing (Program)
AP	Advanced Placement
COA	Cost of attendance
DL	Direct loan
EA	Early action
ED	Early decision
EFC	Expected Family Contribution
FAA	Financial aid administrator
FAFSA	Free Application for Federal Student Aid
FFEL	Federal Family Education Loan
FSEOG	Federal Supplemental Educational Opportunity Grant
FWS	Federal Work Study
PLUS	Parent Loan for Undergraduate Students
PSAT	Preliminary Standardized Aptitude Test
SAR	Student Aid Report
SAT	Standardized Aptitude Test

Deferred enrollment A deferment, offered by most colleges, which permits students to postpone enrollment for up to one year and still have a place at the college.
WHAT IT MEANS TO YOU: Eurail pass, anyone?

Early action (EA) A nonbinding program in which you can apply early and receive an early decision in December, but you do not have to notify the college of your decision until the standard candidate reply date in May.
WHAT IT MEANS TO YOU: A no brainer. Absolutely do this.

Early decision (ED) A binding program in which you can apply to one school early and receive a decision in December. If you are accepted, you must attend.
WHAT IT MEANS TO YOU: A bad idea unless you are absolutely certain you want to attend that school and you definitely do not need any financial aid.

Expected Family Contribution (EFC) This is the amount, as determined by your FAFSA, that your family is expected to contribute to your tuition.
WHAT IT MEANS TO YOU: If you're looking for federal loans and grants, hope this figure is low.

FAFSA (Free Application for Federal Aid) A form you submit to the federal government (you can fill it out electronically) with your and your family's financial information. The government uses the information to inform the college how much financial aid you need. You should submit the FAFSA the January before you begin college.
WHAT IT MEANS TO YOU: Mandatory paperwork if you want financial aid.

Federal Family Education Loans (FFEL) Funds for this type of loan, also called Stafford Loans, are provided by private lenders, not the government.
WHAT IT MEANS TO YOU: These private lenders will be taking checks from you long after you've graduated. Choose wisely.

Federal methodology This is the formula used by the government to calculate your expected family contribution.
WHAT IT MEANS TO YOU: This determines what type of aid you can get from the government.

Federal Pell Grant This is a need-based financial award of up to $4,050 given to undergraduates. The government provides schools with the funds to award all eligible students with the maximum amount of money they qualify for. Since this is a grant, not a loan, it does not have to be repaid.
WHAT IT MEANS TO YOU: If you're eligible, it's free tuition money.

Financial aid A combination of grants, loans, and scholarships that helps students pay for college.
WHAT IT MEANS TO YOU: If you're like a lot of students, it's how you pay for your four-year education extravaganza.

Financial need This is the difference between the cost of tuition and your EFC (expected family contribution).
WHAT IT MEANS TO YOU: Hope for a grant or scholarship, but look into loans.

529 savings plans A state-run savings plan.
WHAT IT MEANS TO YOU: Talk to a financial adviser before opening one. This can increase your EFC (expected family contribution).

Grants Grants are need-based financial awards that don't have to be repaid.
WHAT IT MEANS TO YOU: If you're eligible, go after them.

Institutional methodology This is the formula used by colleges to determine your expected family contribution. It's based on your CSS PROFILE.
WHAT IT MEANS TO YOU: This is what colleges use to figure out how much aid you'll receive.

Ivy League A term that has become synonymous with elite educational standards, the Ivy League is a sports conference made up of eight universities in the Northeast (Brown, Columbia, Cornell, Dartmouth, Harvard, Princeton, Penn, and Yale).
WHAT IT MEANS TO YOU: Very little, unless you are one of the select few who will be accepted into one of these schools.

Lifetime learning credit An annual tax credit of up to $2,000 you can claim to offset the costs of your college tuition.
WHAT IT MEANS TO YOU: A lot of paperwork, but a credit of up to $2,000 per year.

Merit-based aid Merit-based aid is a financial award given in the form of a scholarship to a student with a special talent or achievement in academics, art, athletics, or music.
WHAT IT MEANS TO YOU: It's a great deal if you can get it.

National Merit Scholarship Program This is an academic competition in which you can receive merit-based (as opposed to need-based) scholarship money. You must take the PSAT to qualify.
WHAT IT MEANS TO YOU: You should take the PSAT anyway to practice for the SAT.

Need-blind admissions A need-blind admissions policy means that a school does not factor in an applicant's financial need when deciding which applicants to accept. Brown, Duke, Georgetown, MIT, Stanford, and Yale are a few of the schools that operate according to this policy. (Without need-blind admissions, colleges tend to accept mostly students [within the qualified applicant pool] who can pay the full tuition.)
WHAT IT MEANS TO YOU: It's a great idea in theory. But not everyone is convinced that schools stick to this policy.

Online applications As the name suggests, online applications are submitted over the Internet.
WHAT IT MEANS TO YOU: You get to bypass the U. S. Postal Service. But be sure to print out your application and proofread it carefully before you hit the send button.

Online learning Online learning, also called distance learning, refers to classes offered online instead of at a university. Getting into an online course at a college is significantly easier than being accepted through the normal channels.
WHAT IT MEANS TO YOU: No parties. But maybe that Ivy degree isn't so impossible after all.

Open admissions Open admissions is an enrollment system in which a school, often a community college, accepts applicants without regard to academic qualifications.
WHAT IT MEANS TO YOU: Junior college.

Perkins Loan A federal low-interest loan of up to $4,000 per year that is awarded to students with the greatest financial need.
WHAT IT MEANS TO YOU: You have to qualify. And you have to pay it back.

PLAN This test serves as an excellent practice run for the ACT. It is typically administered to tenth graders.
WHAT IT MEANS TO YOU: If you plan on taking the ACT, take the PLAN to prepare.

PLUS Loan A PLUS Loan (Parent Loan for Undergraduate Students) is a federal loan your parents can take out to help pay for your education. It is based on your parents' credit history, rather than on need. PLUS Loans can be obtained through the FFELP (Federal Family Education Loan Program) or the Direct Loan Program.
WHAT IT MEANS TO YOU: Your parents take out the loan, not you.

Preferential packaging This is a financial aid term that means that universities offer the best financial aid packages to students at the top of their applicant pool.
WHAT IT MEANS TO YOU: It's a good idea to apply to at least one school where you will be a top applicant, if only so you can use that financial aid package to negotiate for a better deal from other schools.

PSAT Also known as the National Merit Scholarship Qualifying Test, this test serves as an excellent practice run for the SAT, and your score doesn't get reported to colleges.
WHAT IT MEANS TO YOU: It's one Saturday morning — take the test.

Regular decision This is the standard method of applying to college. Applications are due in January or February, and decisions are mailed out in April.
WHAT IT MEANS TO YOU: Nail-biting in April along with other seniors across the country. But it's the way to go if you don't have a clear first choice, and/or are hoping for financial aid.

Rolling admissions First come, first served is the idea behind this admissions system. There is no final deadline in rolling admissions. Schools continue to accept students as they apply until all of the spaces are filled.
WHAT IT MEANS TO YOU: These are usually your backup schools.

SAR (Student Aid Report) This is the report sent to you by the federal government that tells you how much money your family is expected to pay toward your tuition — your EFC (Expected Family Contribution). This amount is based on the information you provide in your FAFSA (Free Application for Federal Student Aid).
WHAT IT MEANS TO YOU: Unless money is not an issue, hope for a low figure.

SAT I (New SAT) The end-all, be-all of standardized tests, the SAT is the college entrance exam most commonly used by the more competitive colleges and colleges on the coasts. (Almost all colleges now accept the ACT in its place.) The New SAT has three sections: math, critical reading, and writing. A perfect score is 2400.
WHAT IT MEANS TO YOU: If you haven't already, start learning those vocab words.

SAT Subject Tests (SAT II) Subject tests are one-hour standardized tests administered in 20 different subjects. Many of the more competitive universities usually require applicants to submit a minimum of three subject tests.
WHAT IT MEANS TO YOU: Take these tests in June, right after you finish the course, when all the information is still fresh in your brain.

Scholarships Scholarships are merit-based awards given to students with special talent or achievement in the fields of academics, art, athletics, music, and leadership.
WHAT IT MEANS TO YOU: It's a great deal if you can get one.

Single-choice early action Under this policy, you are allowed to apply early action to only one school. (Harvard, Stanford, and Yale use this policy.) However, your application is not binding, as it would be with early decision.
WHAT IT MEANS TO YOU: It beats early decision, but it's not as good as plain old early action.

Subsidized loan This is a type of loan given only to students with proven financial need, in which the government pays the interest on your loan while you attend college.
WHAT IT MEANS TO YOU: It beats the alternative.

Transcript This is a copy of a student's academic record, sent out as part of the college admissions process.
WHAT IT MEANS TO YOU: Make every grade count.

Unsubsidized loan This is a type of loan in which you owe the interest for the time that you are in school. If you do not have proven financial need, this is the type of loan you will get.
WHAT IT MEANS TO YOU: You'll owe more money.

Weighted GPA This is a modified grading scale of 1 to 5 for academically rigorous courses such as AP classes, as opposed to the standard 1 to 4 scale. It means honors students can surpass a 4.0.
WHAT IT MEANS TO YOU: Study hard and try to break a 4.0.

INDEX

Page numbers in bold indicate worksheets.